TOEIC® LISTENING AND READING TEST 標準模試 1

神崎正哉
Daniel Warriner

yadokari

TOEIC is a registered trademark of Educational Testing Service (ETS). This publication is not endorsed or approved by ETS.

はじめに

　2016年5月の公開テストでTOEIC Listening & Reading Testが10年ぶりに改訂されました。主な変更点は以下の通りです。

- パート1、2、5の問題数が減り、その分パート3、6、7が増えた。
- パート3に3人の話者による会話が加わった。
- パート3、4に図表を見て答える問題が加わった。
- パート3、4、7にある文の文脈中の意味を問う問題が加わった。
- パート6に選択肢が文になっている問題が加わった。
- パート7でオンライン・チャットが使われるようになった。
- パート7に、ある文を入れるのに適切な場所を選ぶ問題が加わった。
- パート7で関連する3文書を読んで設問に答える問題が使われるようになった。

　比較的に解きやすいパート1、2、5の問題数が減り、難しめのパート3、6、7の問題数が増えました。新たに加わる新形式問題は小手先のテクニックが通用しない手強い問題なので、全体の難易度は上がるだろうと予想して、前作の『TOEIC® TEST新形式模試 はじめての挑戦』は難易度をかなり高めに設定しました。しかし、実際に新形式問題のテストが始まってみると、さほど難易度は上がりませんでした。2016年5月と6月の公開テストは易しく、それに比べると7月の公開テストは難しめでしたが、9月はまた易しくなりました。しかしながら、初中級者に限らず、上級者でも「パート3の話者が3人の問題が聞き取りにくい」「パート7の分量が多くなった」という声があることも事実です。また、文脈を理解しないと解けない問題が多くなった分、受験者の負担が上がりました。本書では、そのような傾向を踏まえ、問題のレベルを本番のテストと同じレベルに設定しました。もちろん、使用語彙や問われるポイントも本番に合わせてあります。

　スコアアップのために一番有効な学習は、模試を使ったトレーニングです。良質な模試を繰り返し解いて、テストに対応できる時間感覚を養ってください。そして、やりっぱなしにするのではなく、間違えた問題をしっかり見直してください。そして後日、復習も忘れずに。本書の問題は、選択肢も含めて本番のテストに対応しており、繰り返しトレーニングするに耐え得る問題です。学習の具体的な進め方は、「本書の使い方」で詳しく説明していますので、そちらをご覧ください。

　また、本書ではリーディング問題の読み上げ音声も用意してあります。リーディング問題の復習がリスニングの練習にもなります。

　本書がみなさまのTOEICスコアアップの一助になることを願っています。

2016年11月
神崎正哉

もくじ

はじめに 2
本書の使い方 4
スマートフォンアプリの活用法 6

▶ 新形式模試

Part 1 8
Part 2 12
Part 3 13
Part 4 17
Part 5 20
Part 6 23
Part 7 27

▶ 解答・解説

解答一覧 50
予想スコア換算表 51
Part 1 52
Part 2 54
Part 3 60
Part 4 86
Part 5 106
Part 6 114
Part 7 122

解答用紙 173
文法用語まとめ 174

著者紹介 175

本書の使い方

本書の音声ダウンロードにつきましては、yadokariホームページにて詳細をご案内しております。メニューの「音声ダウンロード」をご参照ください。

 www.yadokari-pub.com

また、本書は、TOEIC自動採点・分析アプリabceed analyticsと提携しています。スマートフォンで簡単に「自動採点・分析・音声再生」が可能です。あわせてご活用ください。

www.globeejapan.com

▶ トレーニングの方法

1 時間を測って制限時間内に200問解く練習をする

TOEICは2時間で200問を解く試験です。実際の試験と同じ制限時間内に200問まとめて解くことで、試験のペース配分がわかります。特にリーディングの問題は、時間配分が重要です。どのくらいのスピードで解き進めればよいか知るために時間を測って解く練習が大変効果的です。

また、TOEICでは2時間集中力を維持させる持久力も必要です。2時間集中してTOEICの問題を解くことで「TOEIC持久力」を養うことができます。初めは集中力が続かない人でも、2時間で200問解く練習を繰り返しやっていると徐々に持久力が付いていきます。

2 正解の根拠を確認する

問題を解き終わったら、答えの確認をしてください。そして、間違えた問題、何となくよさそうだと思って選び正解していた問題、ともに正解の根拠をきちんと確認してください。正解の理由がわかれば、次に同じような問題に出会った時、正解を選べます。正解の根拠がよくわかっていないと、次に同じような問題を解く時、また同じ間違えを繰り返してしまいます。

TOEICでは、毎回、同じような問題が出題されます。本番で同じ間違えを繰り返さなければ、スコアは上がります。ですから、正解の根拠の確認がスコアアップの鍵になるのです。

3 問題中に出てきた知らない語句を覚える

問題中で知らない語句が使われていたら、意味を調べて覚えてください。答えに絡まない部分で使われていた語句であってもしっかり覚えましょう。次に受ける試験では、その語句が問われるかもしれません。例えば次のような問題を模試で解いたとします。

101. Market research analysts pointed out that the most successful vendors offer products that are tailored to the specific needs of ------- customers.

(A) they
(B) their
(C) them
(D) themselves

　この問題は、空所の後ろにcustomersという名詞が続いているので、(B) theirが正解になるという基本的な問題です。しかし、この文にはanalysts、successful、vendors、tailored、specificなどのパート5の語彙問題で出題されてもおかしくない語が含まれています。
　これらの語の意味を確認してしっかり覚えるか、わからないまま放置するかで、今後のスコアの伸びに大きな差がつきます。

4 朗読音声を活用し、音の練習をする

　リーディング問題を含めた朗読音声を活用してトレーニングをするとリスニング力が上がります。英語の音の特徴（音がつながる、消える、弱くなるなど）を意識して、聞こえた音を真似して声に出してみてください。その際、リズムやイントネーションも真似るようにしましょう。声に出す練習は、場面を想像して、その人物になりきってやると効果があります。また、意味を感じながらやると英語が体によく染み込みます。以下のような練習法があります。

▶ **リッスン＆リピート**……音声を聞いて、聞こえた通りに真似して声に出す。パート1やパート2の短い文を使うとやりやすい。スクリプトを見ないでやった方が効果的だが、難しい場合はスクリプトを見てもよい。

▶ **オーバーラッピング**……音声を流して、スクリプトを見ながら、同時進行で声に出して読み進める。

▶ **シャドーイング**…………音声を流して、スクリプトを見ないで、英文の後について声に出す（音声は止めない）。

　また、パート3の会話とパート4のトークの暗唱もスコアアップに役立ちます。暗唱は、(1) 意味を確認する、(2) 音を確認する、(3) 何回も声に出して読んで覚える、の3ステップで行うのがよいでしょう。TOEICで使われる会話・トークは、場面設定、話の流れ、使われている語句が似ているので、ある程度の数を覚えると、本番で似たようなものに出会う確率が高まります。自分が暗唱した会話・トークと似たものが本番に出たら、理解しやすいはずです。

本書の問題は全問、繰り返し復習トレーニングをするに足る鍛えられた良問です。信じて実践してください。必ず、スコアは上がります。

スマートフォンアプリの活用法

音声が、スマートフォンの無料アプリabceed analyticsで、簡単に聴けるようになりました。

　語学は、短い時間でも、毎日繰り返し触れることが上達の秘訣です。
　同じ学習教材を1度解いただけでは、記憶の定着率が低いことが、科学的もわかっています。「学習後、1日後には学習の約33パーセント、6日後には約25パーセント、1カ月後には約21パーセントしか覚えていることができない」ということを「エビンハウスの忘却曲線」は示しています。つまり、同じ30分の学習をするにしても、30分まとめてやるよりも、

> 1回目　6分
> 2回目　数時間後に6分
> 3回目　1日後に6分
> 4回目　2日後に6分
> 5回目　1週間後に6分

と間隔を置いて学習したほうが、効果は数段上がります。
　そこで、忙しい学習者にとって重要となるのが、電車の通勤時間など、「細切れの時間」の活用です。
　たとえば、満員電車でテキストを広げるスペースがないような状況でも、

「一度解いて（間違えた箇所を）見直した問題の朗読音声を聴く」
「リーディング問題であっても、リスニング問題のように文脈をたどりながら聴く」

というようなトレーニングは可能です。もし、わからない箇所があったら、あとで確認すればいいのです。「細切れ」であっても密度の濃いトレーニングになります。また、どんな場所でも英語を聴き取る集中力をつけることができます。
　もちろん、「毎日寝る前の10分、音声を聴きながらテキストを読む」という学習も大変効果的です。人間の記憶は寝ている間に無意識に再構築されて強化されますから、睡眠直前の学習、というのは特に有効です。

　より手軽に、細切れ時間を使った学習をしていただくことができますように、本書ではスマートフォンの無料アプリのabceed analyticsと提携しました。
　abceed analyticsアプリの最大の特長は、

▶スマートフォンで、簡単に音声を再生できること
▶音声の速度を容易に変えることができること

です。

初級・中級者のなかには、より生の会話に近いパート3など、そのままのスピードでは聴き取りにくい、という方がいらっしゃるかもしれません。その場合は、0.8倍速などに速度を落として練習するのもいいでしょう。それで聴き取れるようになったら、本番と同じ1.0倍速で聴き取れるようにスピードを上げていけばいいのです。

　ノーマルスピードではもの足りないという上級者は、1.2倍速、1.5倍速の「高地トレーニング」も有効です。その速さに慣れておけば、本番のテストでは余裕を持って回答できるようになるはずです。

また、abceed analyticsには、自動採点・分析の機能もついています。

このアプリで模試を解けば、パートごとの正解率が出てきますので、自分の弱いパートがどこなのかもひと目でわかります。

　さらに、自分の間違えた問題がひと目でわかりますので、弱点補強の学習をすることもできます。

　また、解答する時間も記録されますので、どのタイプの問題で時間がかかってしまうのか、自分がどんな時間配分で解いているかがわかります。それを分析、検討して時間を意識したトレーニングしていけば、ご自分に合った時間配分の作戦を立てて本番に臨むことができるでしょう。

また、各問題ごとに、同じアプリを使って学習しているユーザーの正答率も表示されます。特に、正答率の高い問題を落としている人は、何か理由があるはずです。しっかりと問題と向き合って、ご自分の弱点を見きわめましょう。

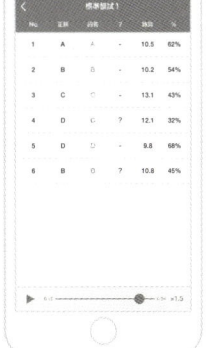

abceed analyticsの自動採点・分析、音声再生アプリは無料で使用できます。
スマートフォンをお持ちの方は、よろしければ試してみてください。

LISTENING TEST

In the Listening test, you will be asked to demonstrate how well you understand spoken English. The entire Listening test will last approximately 45 minutes. There are four parts, and directions are given for each part. You must mark your answers on the separate answer sheet. Do not write your answers in your test book.

PART 1

Directions: For each question in this part, you will hear four statements about a picture in your test book. When you hear the statements, you must select the one statement that best describes what you see in the picture. Then find the number of the question on your answer sheet and mark your answer. The statements will not be printed in your test book and will be spoken only one time.

Statement (C), "They're sitting at a table," is the best description of the picture, so you should select answer (C) and mark it on your answer sheet.

1.

2.

3.

4.

5.

6.

PART 2

Directions: You will hear a question or statement and three responses spoken in English. They will not be printed in your test book and will be spoken only one time. Select the best response to the question or statement and mark the letter (A), (B), or (C) on your answer sheet.

7. Mark your answer on you answer sheet.
8. Mark your answer on you answer sheet.
9. Mark your answer on you answer sheet.
10. Mark your answer on you answer sheet.
11. Mark your answer on you answer sheet.
12. Mark your answer on you answer sheet.
13. Mark your answer on you answer sheet.
14. Mark your answer on you answer sheet.
15. Mark your answer on you answer sheet.
16. Mark your answer on you answer sheet.
17. Mark your answer on you answer sheet.
18. Mark your answer on you answer sheet.
19. Mark your answer on you answer sheet.
20. Mark your answer on you answer sheet.
21. Mark your answer on you answer sheet.
22. Mark your answer on you answer sheet.
23. Mark your answer on you answer sheet.
24. Mark your answer on you answer sheet.
25. Mark your answer on you answer sheet.
26. Mark your answer on you answer sheet.
27. Mark your answer on you answer sheet.
28. Mark your answer on you answer sheet.
29. Mark your answer on you answer sheet.
30. Mark your answer on you answer sheet.
31. Mark your answer on you answer sheet.

PART 3

Directions: You will hear some conversations between two or more people. You will be asked to answer three questions about what the speakers say in each conversation. Select the best response to each question and mark the letter (A), (B), (C), or (D) on your answer sheet. The conversations will not be printed in your test book and will be spoken only one time.

32. Where most likely does the woman work?
    (A) At a construction site
    (B) At a hardware store
    (C) At a shopping mall
    (D) At a shoe store

33. What does the man want to know?
    (A) If a stadium will open soon
    (B) If some hardware is required
    (C) If a type of product is available
    (D) If an event has already started

34. What does the man say he will do tomorrow?
    (A) Visit a nearby business
    (B) Start a new job
    (C) Submit an application form
    (D) Buy a uniform

35. What type of business are the speakers planning to open?
    (A) A parking garage
    (B) A catering company
    (C) A car dealership
    (D) A grocery store

36. Why is the man concerned?
    (A) An area might be too small.
    (B) A sale might be finished.
    (C) A customer might be late.
    (D) A business might be closed.

37. What does one of the women offer to do?
    (A) Send some cards
    (B) Move some cars
    (C) Place some orders
    (D) Buy some food

38. What has the woman been looking for?
    (A) A room
    (B) A device
    (C) A coworker
    (D) A record

39. What does the woman tell the man?
    (A) She checked two rooms.
    (B) She had a technical problem.
    (C) She looked for an item in a store.
    (D) She could not present a report.

40. What does the man suggest the woman do?
    (A) Attend a presentation
    (B) Postpone a project
    (C) Contact a coworker
    (D) Review some data

41. Why does the man talk to the woman?
    (A) To offer some assistance
    (B) To discuss a research project
    (C) To find out about a conference
    (D) To register for some workshops

42. What does the woman suggest the man do?
    (A) Read a blog
    (B) Verify some information
    (C) Change a design
    (D) Attend a conference

43. What is the woman interested in doing?
    (A) Taking photographs
    (B) Designing a blog
    (C) Entering a contest
    (D) Joining a project

GO ON TO THE NEXT PAGE

44. What is the purpose of the call?
  (A) To cancel an appointment
  (B) To see if an error was made
  (C) To ask if an item was found
  (D) To reschedule a delivery

45. Why did the woman fill out a form?
  (A) To report a change of address
  (B) To order some travel accessories
  (C) To put a subscription on hold
  (D) To book accommodation

46. What does the man offer to do today?
  (A) Deliver a newspaper
  (B) Provide some instructions
  (C) Prepare a new form
  (D) Accept a submission

47. Why is the woman calling?
  (A) To confirm a payment
  (B) To make an additional reservation
  (C) To correct a billing error
  (D) To request a form

48. What does the woman tell the man?
  (A) She is trying to calculate a total.
  (B) She is arranging to stay with a relative.
  (C) She is expecting to arrive on a later date.
  (D) She is planning to purchase two books.

49. What does the man offer to do?
  (A) Provide a registration form
  (B) Make a recommendation
  (C) Send a message
  (D) Refund a deposit

50. What does the man want the woman to copy?
  (A) A schedule
  (B) A floor plan
  (C) A handout
  (D) A sales contract

51. What is the problem?
  (A) A file has been damaged.
  (B) A meeting has already ended.
  (C) Some paper is the wrong size.
  (D) Some information is incomplete.

52. What does the woman agree to do?
  (A) Update a document
  (B) Make thirty-two copies
  (C) Participate in a meeting
  (D) Go to another floor

53. Why does the woman apologize to the man?
  (A) She left the door to the room open.
  (B) She believes that she made a mistake.
  (C) She has not finished an assignment.
  (D) She thinks that she has interrupted him.

54. What does the man mean when he says, "I'll see to that in a moment"?
  (A) He will look through some mail.
  (B) He will check an advertisement.
  (C) He will take away some flyers.
  (D) He will post a notice in a room.

55. According to the woman, how is some information protected?
  (A) By restricting access to an area
  (B) By regularly changing a password
  (C) By having a guard on duty
  (D) By keeping it in one place

56. What does the woman say will happen tomorrow?
    (A) A new employee will start a job.
    (B) A business will open at ten o'clock.
    (C) A technician will give a presentation.
    (D) A manager will order some tools.

57. Where most likely are the speakers?
    (A) At a newspaper
    (B) At an auto repair shop
    (C) At a travel agency
    (D) At a technical school

58. What must Raymond do by ten o'clock?
    (A) Introduce a system
    (B) Make a repair
    (C) Sign a contract
    (D) Arrange some tools

59. Why does the woman say, "I know just what you mean"?
    (A) She feels the same way as the man.
    (B) She would like some more details.
    (C) She understands the steps in a process.
    (D) She has already heard what happened.

60. Why is the man concerned?
    (A) A customer might complain.
    (B) The weather may get worse.
    (C) Someone could be injured.
    (D) Some snow is too deep.

61. What does the woman suggest they do?
    (A) Close an entrance
    (B) Wash some steps
    (C) Bring some shovels
    (D) Get a sign

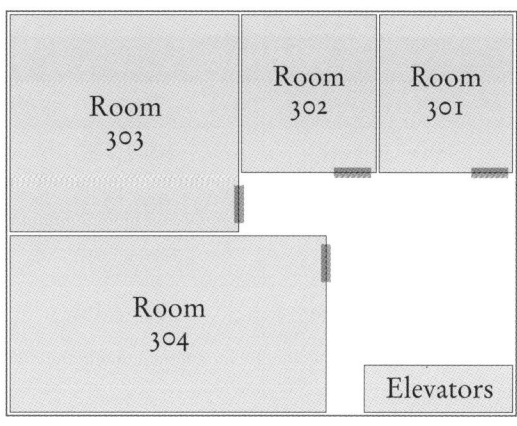

62. What does the man say about the big room?
    (A) It is occupied.
    (B) It is decorated.
    (C) It is comfortable.
    (D) It is unlocked.

63. Look at the graphic. Which room will the speakers paint first?
    (A) Room 301
    (B) Room 302
    (C) Room 303
    (D) Room 304

64. What does the man want to do?
    (A) Cover some furniture
    (B) Wait for a manager
    (C) Check a guest book
    (D) Remove some plastic

GO ON TO THE NEXT PAGE

SEMINARS	
LEADER	TIME
John Higgins	9:30–10:50
Derrick Hunter	11:00–12:30
Lunch	12:30–1:00
Pamela Plummer	1:00–2:45
David Robinson	3:00–4:45

WREN'S GYM
3887 SW King Ave., Portland, OR

$6.00 OFF an Aerobics Class

Anyone can join!
Valid Monday thru Friday.
Coupon can be used only once.

65. Why does the man want to start immediately?
    (A) They have a number of topics to discuss.
    (B) A registration deadline is approaching.
    (C) He has to attend another meeting.
    (D) They are expected in a seminar room before 9:30.

66. What does the woman bring to the man's attention?
    (A) A topic is not on an agenda.
    (B) A product launch needs to be discussed first.
    (C) There is an error on a Web site.
    (D) Some seminars may take longer than planned.

67. Look at the graphic. Who will lead a seminar starting at one o'clock?
    (A) Mr. Higgins
    (B) Mr. Hunter
    (C) Ms. Plummer
    (D) Mr. Robinson

68. Why is the woman surprised?
    (A) Her membership has expired.
    (B) The health club is busy.
    (C) A class was cancelled.
    (D) The man still remembers her.

69. Look at the graphic. Why is the woman unable to use the coupon?
    (A) It is for a different type of class.
    (B) She has already used the coupon once.
    (C) She must first renew her membership.
    (D) It is not valid on Saturday.

70. What does the man say the woman can do?
    (A) See a price list
    (B) Sign up for another class
    (C) Avoid some charges
    (D) Take a class schedule

PART 4

Directions: You will hear some talks given by a single speaker. You will be asked to answer three questions about what the speaker says in each talk. Select the best response to each question and mark the letter (A), (B), (C), or (D) on your answer sheet. The talks will not be printed in your test book and will be spoken only one time.

71. Where is the speaker calling from?
    (A) An office building
    (B) An airport
    (C) A café
    (D) A train station

72. What time will the woman probably leave for Birmingham?
    (A) At 6:15
    (B) At 7:30
    (C) At 1:00
    (D) At 2:00

73. What does the speaker plan to do in Birmingham?
    (A) Dine with a client
    (B) Stay at a hotel
    (C) Give a presentation
    (D) Inspect a building

74. What is the main purpose of the talk?
    (A) To report some mistakes
    (B) To announce a job opportunity
    (C) To introduce a guest speaker
    (D) To provide some instructions

75. According to the speaker, what will happen soon?
    (A) Some machine parts will be installed.
    (B) Mr. Arnolds will give a demonstration.
    (C) The listeners will look at a drawing of a facility.
    (D) An illustration will be displayed on a screen.

76. What does the speaker ask the listeners to do?
    (A) Operate a machine
    (B) Complete a list
    (C) Unwrap a package
    (D) Share a manual

77. What does the speaker announce?
    (A) A magazine launch
    (B) A publishing date
    (C) A new tourist destination
    (D) A ranking of cities

78. Where is the broadcast being made?
    (A) Abura
    (B) Huntston
    (C) Portgomery
    (D) Irving

79. According to the speaker, why should the listeners be proud?
    (A) A local writer won a prize.
    (B) Many tourists have been visiting their city.
    (C) Their city was recognized as a good place to live.
    (D) Their mayor was honored with an award.

80. Who most likely is the speaker?
    (A) A tour guide
    (B) A hotel clerk
    (C) A restaurant owner
    (D) A bus driver

81. Where will the listeners go after lunch?
    (A) To a courthouse
    (B) To a port
    (C) To a store
    (D) To a museum

82. According to the speaker, what can the listeners do?
    (A) View a historical document
    (B) Leave behind personal belongings
    (C) Take pictures inside some shops
    (D) Participate in an activity for free

GO ON TO THE NEXT PAGE

83. What is the main purpose of the event?
   (A) To celebrate the anniversary of a park
   (B) To attract visitors to the area
   (C) To show gratitude to some volunteers
   (D) To prepare for some outdoor projects

84. What does the speaker mean when she says, "and doing much more"?
   (A) The listeners did more work than they were assigned.
   (B) The listeners did a lot more volunteer work this year.
   (C) The listeners are expected to participate again next year.
   (D) The listeners carried out numerous other tasks as well.

85. What will the listeners most likely do next?
   (A) Have a meal
   (B) Move a table
   (C) Help visitors
   (D) Clean dishes

86. Why does the caller apologize?
   (A) A newspaper was delivered to the wrong address.
   (B) An advertisement was not placed as requested.
   (C) A date in an article was incorrect.
   (D) A document was not properly formatted.

87. What does the caller say happened?
   (A) She did not read some information correctly.
   (B) She was told to choose a date in February.
   (C) She met with Mr. Meredith on a Saturday.
   (D) She was unable to fill out a form completely.

88. What is the caller offering?
   (A) Subscription discounts
   (B) Free advertising space
   (C) Copies of a newspaper
   (D) Design suggestions

89. What type of business is being advertised?
   (A) A seaside resort
   (B) A home improvement store
   (C) A construction company
   (D) A real estate agency

90. According to the advertisement, what do people like the most about the business?
   (A) Its employees
   (B) Its selection
   (C) Its location
   (D) Its prices

91. What does the speaker mean when he says, "Need I say more"?
   (A) He cannot reveal a secret.
   (B) He wants to describe the business more.
   (C) He feels that he has mentioned enough.
   (D) He would like to repeat some information.

92. What is the purpose of the announcement?
   (A) To promote a talk
   (B) To explain a technique
   (C) To describe a job
   (D) To report a delay

93. Why will Mr. Bennet be using a different room?
   (A) A screen was set up in the wrong place.
   (B) Some sessions were not scheduled correctly.
   (C) Some equipment is not working properly.
   (D) A hall is not big enough for an audience.

94. What does the speaker mean when she says, "don't miss out"?
   (A) Listeners should listen carefully.
   (B) Listeners should attend a lecture.
   (C) Listeners should not forget some advice.
   (D) Listeners should not be unhappy.

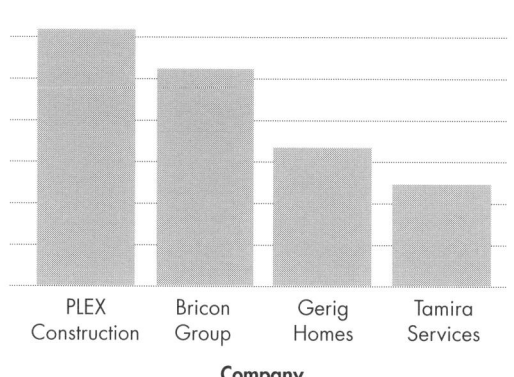

Sales in September

Ludlow Bay Ferries
MORNING DEPARTURE TIMES

Eastbound Ferry	Westbound Ferry
7:10	7:40
8:10	8:40
9:20	10:00
10:40	11:20

95. Why did Mr. Hewitt call the Sales Department?
    (A) To discuss a billing error
    (B) To complain about a shipment
    (C) To order additional materials
    (D) To inquire about product features

96. Look at the graphic. Which company does Mr. Hewitt work for?
    (A) PLEX Construction
    (B) Bricon Group
    (C) Gerig Homes
    (D) Tamira Services

97. What does the speaker tell listeners to do?
    (A) Speak directly to construction site supervisors
    (B) Keep accurate records of warehouse inventory
    (C) Ensure that all shipments are checked twice
    (D) Correct errors in some recent sales data

98. What problem does the speaker announce?
    (A) A bus is running late.
    (B) A ticket machine is broken.
    (C) A tour has been cancelled.
    (D) A ferry could not leave.

99. According to the speaker, what can some people do?
    (A) Get their money back
    (B) Transfer to a train
    (C) Receive a complimentary ticket
    (D) Reach a destination faster

100. Look at the graphic. What time will the next Eastbound Ferry depart?
    (A) At 7:10
    (B) At 8:10
    (C) At 9:20
    (D) At 10:40

This is the end of the Listening test. Turn to Part 5 in your test book.

READING TEST

In the Reading test, you will read a variety of texts and answer several different types of reading comprehension questions. The entire Reading test will last 75 minutes. There are three parts, and directions are given for each part. You are encouraged to answer as many questions as possible within the time allowed.

You must mark your answers on the separate answer sheet. Do not write your answers in your test book.

PART 5

Directions: A word or phrase is missing in each of the sentences below. Four answer choices are given below each sentence. Select the best answer to complete the sentence. Then mark the letter (A), (B), (C), or (D) on your answer sheet.

---

101. The car manufacturer announced that its convertible will not be available for purchase ------- early next year.
(A) then
(B) about
(C) until
(D) since

102. Business professionals enroll in courses at the Ofra Institute to enhance skills ------- to their jobs.
(A) relevant
(B) consistent
(C) accountable
(D) significant

103. Visit Wilshire Costume Rentals today ------- our brand-new location in the Magnolia Mall on Westwood Avenue.
(A) to
(B) following
(C) at
(D) before

104. The construction of the building resumed six months after the project was suspended ------- a lack of funding.
(A) as much as
(B) even so
(C) as soon as
(D) due to

105. Archways Hotel preferred guests can enjoy ------- use of the fitness centers at all locations.
(A) free
(B) freeing
(C) freed
(D) freedom

106. Any employees ------- are interested in the supervisor position may now submit an application.
(A) whose
(B) who
(C) whoever
(D) whichever

107. The presentations at the symposium featured the world's leading experts on cyber security, ------- Brennen Clayton.
(A) including
(B) performing
(C) regarding
(D) consisting

108. Ms. Browning sold her house without the ------- of a real estate agent.
(A) support
(B) supportive
(C) supporting
(D) supported

109. After forty years ------- the Kendlewood Public Library, librarian Michael McConnell will be retiring on October 31.
(A) through
(B) above
(C) with
(D) about

110. Five days before the workshop, the organization will start charging a fee for ------- registration.
(A) former
(B) late
(C) behind
(D) latter

111. Graphex design software has gone from being a tool for professionals to a program ------- can use.
(A) whenever
(B) ourselves
(C) anyone
(D) other

112. Montego Grill will be closed from 1:00 P.M. to 6:00 P.M. ------- a private function.
(A) along
(B) by
(C) from
(D) for

113. Even though all the contestants were invited to the awards ceremony, only the winners were in -------.
(A) attended
(B) attendees
(C) attending
(D) attendance

114. If ------- pass is not activated, access to the building will be restricted to the main lobby.
(A) yourself
(B) yours
(C) your
(D) you

115. The manager was impressed at how ------- the new salespeople are about the store's merchandise.
(A) knowledge
(B) knowledgeable
(C) known
(D) knowingly

116. The factory owner released a statement confirming that an investigation into the ------- of the accident was underway.
(A) factor
(B) control
(C) opinion
(D) cause

117. Richard Cooke and his team created the spectacular light show ------- for the Star-Pop concert tour.
(A) specify
(B) specifications
(C) specifying
(D) specifically

118. A study by the Rialto Research Institute ------- that organic pesticides are more effective than their synthetic counterparts.
(A) told
(B) brought
(C) found
(D) took

119. Alana Shah was commissioned to design the memorial on the condition that ------- collaborate with another architect.
(A) she
(B) hers
(C) her
(D) herself

120. Seminar participants will be required to ------- a business plan that outlines the details of their proposed venture.
(A) developer
(B) develop
(C) development
(D) developing

121. City council has introduced stringent maintenance requirements to improve the quality of ------- properties in Brownsville.
(A) renting
(B) rental
(C) rents
(D) rent

122. A notice sent to Mr. Malone informed him that his vehicle ------- was set to expire on September 15.
(A) registration
(B) registered
(C) register
(D) registering

123. Although Ms. Robinson took a taxi from the airport, she usually ------- for the company limousine to pick her up.
(A) decides
(B) arranges
(C) contacts
(D) expects

124. ------- the heavy snowfall, Ms. McFarland set up a conference call with the client instead of driving to his office.
(A) Whether
(B) Given
(C) As of
(D) Except for

125. The redevelopment plan includes building a park between Fillmore Road and Blackridge Street, ------- an orchard is currently located.
(A) where
(B) what
(C) when
(D) which

126. Although the committee has met twice to address the dispute, the members still remain ------- over the issue.
(A) attentive
(B) divided
(C) devoted
(D) opposite

127. Once the plant is ------- operational, it will produce more than fifty thousand bottles per day.
(A) adversely
(B) shortly
(C) fully
(D) carefully

128. The number of visitors to the island is expected ------- significantly after the ferry's service hours are extended.
(A) increased
(B) increases
(C) increasingly
(D) to increase

129. According to *Bizsphere Magazine*, Aerowflight is now ------- the world's ten largest aircraft manufacturers.
(A) among
(B) unless
(C) against
(D) until

130. The CEO acted on the ------- of the finance committee to make more investments.
(A) association
(B) progression
(C) development
(D) recommendation

PART 6

Directions: Read the texts that follow. A word, phrase, or sentence is missing in parts of each text. Four answer choices for each question are given below the text. Select the best answer to complete the text. Then mark the letter (A), (B), (C), or (D) on your answer sheet.

Questions 131–134 refer to the following e-mail.

To: nbrowning@ynrgtech.com
From: ktaylor@xylosystems.com
Date: February 19
Subject: Reference Request

Dear Mr. Browning:

A former employee of your company, Nancy Burroughs, has ------- for a position with our
                                           131.

organization. She provided your name and your e-mail address as a reference. As part of our

recruiting process, I am writing to ask if you would be willing ------- some information about her.
                                           132.

-------. This outlines the duties of the post that Ms. Burroughs has applied for. I would be
133.

grateful if you would comment on her ------- for the post. Any other details you can add would
                      134.

be greatly appreciated.

Thank you.

Kathleen Taylor
Personnel Director
Xylo Systems

---

131. (A) accepted
    (B) applied
    (C) filled
    (D) offered

132. (A) of sharing
    (B) to share
    (C) shared
    (D) to have shared

133. (A) It will be useful in making a hiring decision.
    (B) For example, you can ask about her role.
    (C) We would like a response by February 25.
    (D) A job description is attached to this e-mail.

134. (A) suitable
    (B) suited
    (C) suitably
    (D) suitability

GO ON TO THE NEXT PAGE

Questions 135–138 refer to the following notice.

You are invited to join our new book club. We will be discussing contemporary works of fiction twice a month. Our kick-off meeting will take place at the Brentwood Library on September 28. ------- meetings will be held on the second and fourth Thursday of every month at 7:00 P.M.
135.

The first novel we will be reading is *Fleeting Twilight* by Amos Ballard. -------. The book
136.
is currently available in most bookstores.

------- you are interested in becoming a member of the Brentwood Library Book Club, e-mail
137.
Elton Kesey at ekesey@btdlibrary.org. Please let him know that you are coming ------- enough
138.
chairs and tables can be set up ahead of time.

135. (A) Constant
(B) Repetitive
(C) Consecutive
(D) Subsequent ✓

136. (A) He did attend our previous meeting.
(B) It will be released on October 20.
(C) Participants should read it in advance. ✓
(D) However, the library is closed on Monday.

137. (A) For
(B) Until
(C) If ✓
(D) While

138. (A) in case
(B) so that ✓
(C) whereas
(D) although

Questions 139–142 refer to the following information.

Preordering Transgaia Meals

Transgaia Airways understands that more control over the inflight dining experience is what passengers want. That is ------- we offer the convenience of selecting a meal in advance of flights.
139.

Simply enter your flight booking code on the reservations section of this Web site and then choose the meal option of your -------. Meals can be ordered between ten days and twenty-four hours prior to departure. Confirmation of the selection ------- by e-mail.
140. **141.**

If you have a particular dietary requirement, please let us know. -------. All you have to do is contact your travel consultant or the Transgaia Reservations Office with the special meal request.
142.

139. (A) why ✓
 (B) what
 (C) where
 (D) who

140. (A) preference ✓
 (B) preferable
 (C) preferring
 (D) preferred

141. (A) sends
 (B) was sent
 (C) will be sent ✓
 (D) is sending

142. (A) However, another return flight might not be available.
 (B) We can provide you with a suitable alternative meal. ✓
 (C) There are several procedures you need to follow first.
 (D) One will be sent to you soon after we are informed.

Questions 143–146 refer to the following letter.

Mr. Yun Huan
Aggentek Engineering Ltd.
2477 Minyou Road,
Hsinchu, Taiwan

Dear Mr. Huan:

Clarsight Films has been making photographic films for sixty-two years. In the wake of the digital photography age, however, the company recognized a need to diversify. Therefore, ------- **143.** digital cameras quickly replaced film cameras, we expanded our expertise to other industries.

In a move to represent all of our products and services accurately, we will change our name to Clarsight Technologies. -------. **144.** We would appreciate it if you would bring this to the attention of your accounts department and change your records -------. **145.**

We want to assure you that with our new name we will continue to deliver the same high level of quality you have come ------- from us. **146.** And we look forward to continuing our business relationship with you.

Sincerely,

Gareth Donovan
President, Clarsight Films

143. (A) while
(B) as if
(C) except
(D) unless

144. (A) You are welcome to attend this special event.
(B) The relocation will not impact our partnership.
(C) Please be aware that these are being revised.
(D) The change will become effective on March 1.

145. (A) accordingly
(B) suddenly
(C) practically
(D) regularly

146. (A) expectation
(B) expected
(C) to expect
(D) expectantly

PART 7

Directions: In this part you will read a selection of texts, such as magazine and newspaper articles, e-mails, and instant messages. Each text or set of texts is followed by several questions. Select the best answer for each question and mark the letter (A), (B), (C), or (D) on your answer sheet.

Questions 147–148 refer to the following announcement.

Date: January 12

Announcement for all Sales and Service Staff

Effective February 1, Thomas Salvatore will assume the duties of floor manager at our customer call center in Virginia. He is currently a sales team supervisor at our Kentucky branch, where his assistant, Rita Cockrell, will be taking over his position when he leaves.

Mr. Salvatore has worked at Vastynet for eleven years. Prior to serving as a branch supervisor, he was a member of the project team that introduced our new broadband services in Pennsylvania. His first job with the company was service technician at our Delaware location.

We are very pleased to announce this promotion, and we are confident that Mr. Salvatore will demonstrate effective leadership in his new role.

---

147. What is the main purpose of the announcement?
(A) To encourage staff participation
(B) To promote some new services
(C) To announce a personnel change
(D) To introduce some job openings

148. Where does Mr. Salvatore work now?
(A) In Virginia
(B) In Kentucky
(C) In Pennsylvania
(D) In Delaware

Questions 149–150 refer to the following text message chain.

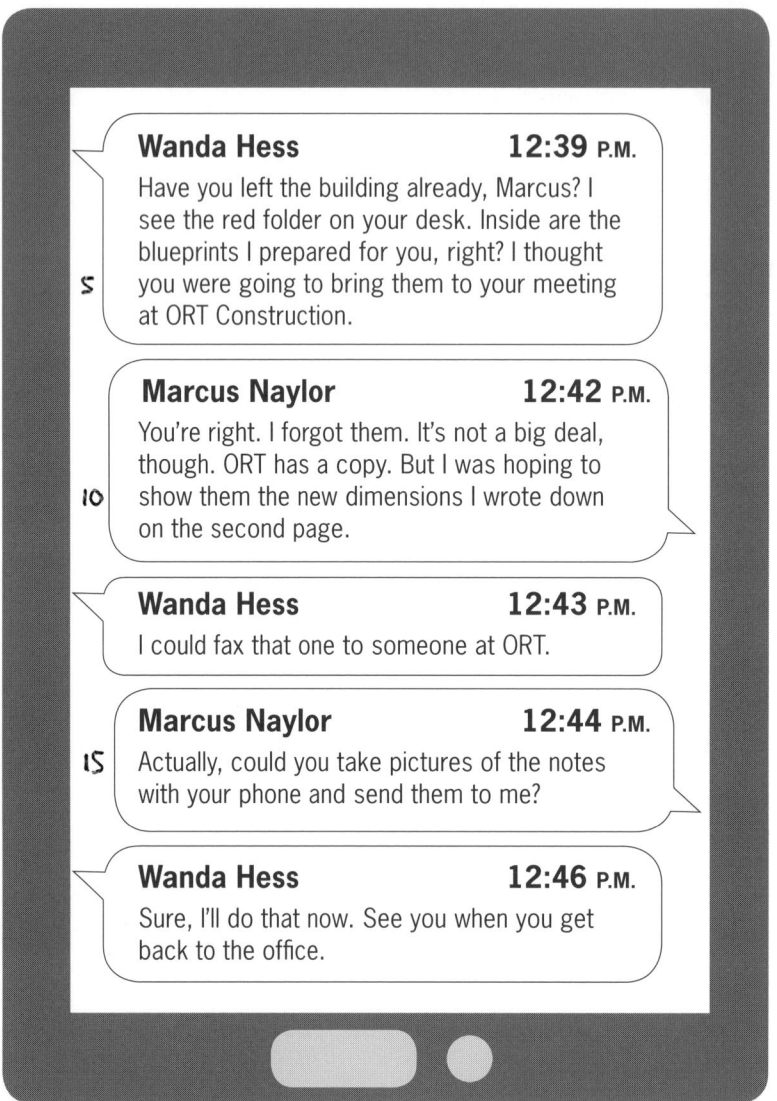

149. At 12:42 P.M., what does Mr. Naylor mean when he writes, "It's not a big deal"?

(A) A meeting is not important.
(B) A contract is not large.
(C) A mistake is not serious.
(D) An agreement is not significant.

150. What does Mr. Naylor ask Ms. Hess to do?

(A) Revise some figures
(B) Send some photographs
(C) Fax a document
(D) Call a client

Questions 151–152 refer to the following notice.

Tuesday Morning Delays

Traks Transit would like to apologize for the disruptions and delays that occurred during morning commute hours on Tuesday, August 26. Service was suspended due to a signal failure caused by an electrical problem on our West District Line. We offered passengers complimentary tickets for subway and bus routes connecting Glendale to the downtown area. Service was restored by 11:10 A.M.

We sincerely apologize for the inconvenience and appreciate your understanding in this matter.

151. Where would the notice most likely appear?
(A) In a bus terminal
(B) In a travel agency
(C) In a train station
(D) In a convenience store

152. What is explained in the notice?
(A) How a device was fixed
(B) Where to get a refund
(C) When a bus departs
(D) Why a service stopped

Questions 153–154 refer to the following letter.

MEADOWS PUBLIC LIBRARY
7644 Apache Drive, Jonesboro, AR 72401

September 29

Timothy Zhang
6438 Access Road
Jonesboro, AR 72397

Dear Mr. Zhang:

The items listed below are overdue. Both of the books should have been returned to the library by September 15. Please bring them to our circulation counter and pay the applicable charges at your earliest convenience.

If you have already brought the items back to the library, we request that you call the Circulation Department at 555-7985 to inform us of the situation.

Thank you in advance for your cooperation.

Circulation Department
Meadows Public Library

Library card holder: Timothy Zhang
Library ID: PIUJDF995835
Accrued fines (to date): $5.60

Title	*Learn to Do Your Own Programming*
Author	Hubert A. Murray
Publisher	Bollinger-Austin Press
Title	*A Beginner's Guide to Computer Programming*
Author	Erik Forester
Publisher	Percipient Publishing Ltd.

153. Why did the library send the letter to Mr. Zhang?
(A) To inform him that books may be picked up
(B) To thank him for making a payment
(C) To request that he return some books
(D) To remind him to renew his library card

154. What can be inferred from the letter?
(A) The library card is enclosed.
(B) The subject of the books is the same.
(C) The library has two branches.
(D) The books were written by the same author.

Questions 155–157 refer to the following receipt.

Ratcliff & Sons
3420 Hillcrest Road
Minneapolis, MN 55401
555-7257

September 18 (3:02 P.M.)
Transaction: 24558
Payment method: OVC Credit Card

Lime Green Latex Paint	$36.70
Cordless Drill	$73.68
Hammer	$19.99
Paint Roller	$28.25
Subtotal	$158.62
Sales Tax	$12.33
Total	$170.95

Bob O'Neil

Cardholder Signature

All return items must be accompanied by a sales receipt and brought back to the store within 30 days of purchase. Only items that are returned in an unused condition and in their original packaging can be accepted. Please be aware that all paints and paint-related products, except for rollers, are non-refundable and cannot be returned to the store for exchange or store credit. Defective electronic devices may be returned for a refund, exchange, or store credit.

CUSTOMER COPY

---

155. Where was the receipt most likely issued?
(A) At a delivery company
(B) At a hardware store
(C) At a post office
(D) At a painting company

156. What is NOT included on the receipt?
(A) A transaction number
(B) The payment method
(C) The time of purchase
(D) A fee for shipping

157. Which item cannot be returned to Ratcliff & Sons?
(A) The lime green latex paint
(B) The cordless drill
(C) The hammer
(D) The paint roller

GO ON TO THE NEXT PAGE

Questions 158–160 refer to the following article.

ARC Hotels Group Announces Plans for Expansion of Coral Bay Resort

Wellington, NZ (23 January)—The ARC Hotels Group has announced plans to expand its Coral Bay resort. The development will include the addition of forty-eight rooms, two restaurants, and a shopping arcade featuring 1,800 square meters of retail space. — [1] —.

The decade-old resort was built next to Anders Grove Golf Club, which ARC purchased last year. — [2] —. The expansion will be constructed on a tract of land adjacent to the golf course.

"Coral Bay has transformed from a quiet coastal village to a tourist hotspot," said Harvey Carter, President, ARC Hotels Group. "Years ago, we saw this change coming, and we wanted our resort there to have more dining options and guest rooms. — [3] —. After purchasing Anders Grove, however, we now have enough land to make it bigger and even better."

The ARC Hotels Group owns 256 hotels around the world, including two in New Zealand. — [4] —. It was founded in 1968 by Samuel Cooper, a businessman who made his fortune in the steel industry. ARC plans to debut its expanded Coral Bay resort in December.

158. What is the article mainly about?
(A) Construction of a golf course
(B) Tourists from overseas
(C) Additions to a resort
(D) Cooperation between two companies

159. What is reported about the ARC Hotels Group?
(A) It plans to open a second hotel on Coral Bay.
(B) It will renovate its headquarters in December.
(C) It is still managed by the founder.
(D) It owns more than one hotel in New Zealand.

160. In which of the positions marked [1], [2], [3], and [4] does the following sentence best belong?

"At the time, this was impossible due to lack of space."

(A) [1]
(B) [2]
(C) [3]
(D) [4]

Questions 161–163 refer to the following information.

Space Available for Rehearsals

Are you looking for a studio to prepare for a performance? Our spacious Sanctum Studio is available to rent by the hour and is conveniently located near the theater district.

Perfect for rehearsals and photo shoots, Sanctum Studio is larger than the average dance studio. Its lobby provides additional space for a piano or other instruments brought to the building.

This multipurpose space also has state-of-the-art sound and lighting equipment and two dressing rooms, which can be used at no additional cost.

DETAILS

Location: 86 Madison Street, Jarviston
Phone: 555-2864

Studio parking: 18-vehicle lot (included in rental rate)
Public parking: parking lot across the street

Pricing: The rate varies depending on the time and day the space is used (standard rate: $45.00 per hour).

A discount is given to students attending Markford College.

To see photographs of Sanctum Studio or to reserve the space online, visit: www.sanctumstudio.org.

161. What is implied about Sanctum Studio?
    (A) It is ideal for practices.
    (B) Its Web site will be redesigned.
    (C) It is usually busy in the evening.
    (D) It is the largest dance studio in Jarviston.

162. What is NOT mentioned as being covered by the rental fee?
    (A) Modern equipment
    (B) Changing rooms
    (C) Parking spaces
    (D) Musical instruments

163. According to the information, what is across the street from Sanctum Studio?
    (A) A university
    (B) A parking lot
    (C) A movie theater
    (D) A public park

GO ON TO THE NEXT PAGE

Questions 164–167 refer to the following form.

Phoenix Grocers
CUSTOMER SERVICE QUESTIONNAIRE

Phoenix Grocers is looking for new ways to make our customers even happier. That is why we want to know how you feel about us. Please take a moment to rate each statement in the list on a scale of 1 to 4, where 1 = strongly agree, 2 = agree, 3 = disagree, and 4 = strongly disagree.

If you include your name and phone number, you will be entered in a drawing for a chance to win 100 dollars' worth of groceries from our store!

Name: _Shania Winston_   Phone: _555-3857_

Statement	1	2	3	4
Phoenix offers more variety than other local supermarkets.	(1)	2	3	4
Phoenix prices are fair compared to those of other supermarkets.	1	(2)	3	4
The produce at Phoenix is always fresh.	(1)	2	3	4
Phoenix employees are helpful.	1	(2)	3	4
Phoenix shelves are well organized.	(1)	2	3	4
There is enough space in the checkout area for bagging groceries.	1	2	(3)	4
I would recommend Phoenix to others.	1	(2)	3	4
Overall, I am satisfied as a Phoenix customer.	1	(2)	3	4

Comments: I regularly visit this supermarket and have noticed it's gotten busier over the years. Getting groceries here used to take 15 minutes, but now it takes half an hour or so. If I were in charge, I'd make space for two more registers.

164. How will Phoenix Grocers most likely use the information it receives on the form?
(A) To determine which products to promote
(B) To increase customer satisfaction
(C) To improve its marketing efforts
(D) To identify hard-working employees

165. What does Ms. Winston indicate on the form?
(A) The selection of products is poor.
(B) Some vegetables are usually sold out.
(C) More shelves should be installed.
(D) There is not enough space in an area.

166. What can be inferred about Ms. Winston?
(A) She walks fifteen minutes to the store every day.
(B) She feels that more cashiers are needed.
(C) She decided not to participate in a drawing.
(D) She prefers to shop at other stores.

167. How has Phoenix Grocers changed?
(A) It offers fewer products.
(B) Its aisles are narrower.
(C) It serves more customers.
(D) Its bags are smaller.

GO ON TO THE NEXT PAGE

Questions 168–171 refer to the following online chat discussion.

Stella Carlson [7:04 P.M.]
Hi all. I want to check if you're ready for tomorrow's assignment. The unveiling will be at Praxra Motors' headquarters at 10:30, right?

Ricky Ross [7:06 P.M.]
Yes, but we should be there before 9:30. The press conference starts at 10:00, and we have to pick up our press passes before that.

Lynn Ramirez [7:07 P.M.]
We'll need time to set up the cameras there, too. I guess we should leave the studio by 8:00.

Clayton Wright [7:09 P.M.]
Lynn and Ricky will be filming the event. Who will be taking pictures of Praxra's new car?

Stella Carlson [7:10 P.M.]
Paul Parker. He couldn't join us for this meeting because he's covering a tennis match for our morning show.

Ricky Ross [7:11 P.M.]
Should I let him know what time we'll be leaving tomorrow?

Stella Carlson [7:12 P.M.]
He'll be here later and I'll be working late, so I'll take care of that. Clayton, have you come up with questions to ask Praxra's president when he gives the press conference?

Clayton Wright [7:13 P.M.]
I'm working on it.

Stella Carlson [7:15 P.M.]
And I'll have to edit the footage tomorrow afternoon. OK, that's it. See you tomorrow.

168. For what type of organization do the writers most likely work?
 (A) A conference center
 (B) A news agency ✓
 (C) A sports arena
 (D) A car manufacturer

169. According to the discussion, what will Mr. Parker do tomorrow?
 (A) Work late
 (B) Take pictures ✓
 (C) Edit videos
 (D) Ask questions

170. When will the president of Praxra Motors speak?
 (A) At 8:00
 (B) At 9:30
 (C) At 10:00 ✓
 (D) At 10:30

171. At 7:13 P.M., what does Mr. Wright mean when he writes, "I'm working on it"?
 (A) He has not finished preparing questions. ✓
 (B) He is editing a story about a tennis match.
 (C) He is unable to answer Ms. Carlson's question.
 (D) He will submit a document later today.

Questions 172–175 refer to the following letter.

February 16

Dr. Annette Weisman
Ceres Institute of Botany Research
935 Hillcrest Road
Glendora, CA 91741

Global Nutrition Research Conference

Dear Dr. Weisman:

On behalf of the Global Nutrition Research Conference (GNRC) committee, it is my pleasure to invite you to participate as a speaker at our event this year. — [1] —. The GNRC will be held in Zurich, Switzerland at the Kallendorf Hotel from June 12 to 15.

Nutrition experts from around the world will gather at the GNRC to discuss a broad range of topics related to the theme "Nutrition for a Healthier Tomorrow." Your research on nutrients in mushrooms that was recently published in the journal *Agricultural Science and Sustainability* will be of interest to many conference attendees. — [2] —.

In addition, your former colleague, Dr. Farida Patel, will give a presentation at the GNRC. On the second day of the event, she will discuss her research on a species of mushroom newly discovered in India. Should you also agree to participate, we will schedule your talk for the following day. — [3] —.

Enclosed you will find a conference information package for invited speakers, which contains a description of the conference and its goals, a guest speaker registration form, our speaker compensation policy, and information about hotels and transportation. — [4] —. If you are interested in being a speaker at the conference, please complete the form and send it to the GNRC Committee Office by March 22.

Yours sincerely,

Dennis Hancock

Dennis Hancock
Executive Director
Global Nutrition Research Conference

172. When does Mr. Hancock want Dr. Weisman to speak at the event?

(A) On June 12
(B) On June 13
(C) On June 14
(D) On June 15

173. What is NOT being sent with the letter?

(A) A conference schedule
(B) Accommodation information
(C) The objectives of the event
(D) A document for registration

174. What is Dr. Weisman asked to do?

(A) Continue her research in another country
(B) Collaborate with a former colleague
(C) Review an article in a scientific journal
(D) Return a document to a committee

175. In which of the positions marked [1], [2], [3], and [4] does the following sentence best belong?

"Moreover, it fits well with the conference theme."

(A) [1]
(B) [2]
(C) [3]
(D) [4]

GO ON TO THE NEXT PAGE

Questions 176–180 refer to the following form and letter.

STAR PARKING
Corner of Lincoln Avenue and Eagle Road

RENTAL AGREEMENT

Owner: Barry Klein
Telephone: 555-9346
Address: 894 Eagle Road, Albertville, MN 55301

Renter: Heidi Welch
Telephone: 555-3867
Address: 9689 Lincoln Avenue, Albertville, MN 55301

The owner agrees to rent Star Parking space __12-F__ to the renter on a month-to-month basis. Prior to each rental month, the renter will pay the rental fee of $50.00 to the owner by check or in cash. The owner will issue a receipt stating the amount paid. In addition to the rental fee, the renter will pay a deposit of $50.00 at the time of signing this agreement. After the final rental month, the owner will return the deposit by check to the renter if no outstanding rent is due. The owner is not responsible for the vehicle while it is parked in the designated space.

Date of agreement: October 29
Signature of owner: Barry Klein
Signature of renter: Heidi Welch

March 27

Barry Klein
894 Eagle Road
Albertville, MN 55301

Dear Mr. Klein:

I currently rent space 12-F at Star Parking. I have accepted a job in Vermont and will move to Burlington on April 30; therefore, the enclosed payment for rental of the space will be my last.

As of May 1, my home address will be 412 Cherry Street, Burlington, VT 05401. Since I will be leaving Albertville on April 30, please mail the check for fifty dollars to my new address.

Thank you for always ensuring that the parking lot remains clear of snow in the winter and well lit at night year-round.

Best regards,

Heidi Welch

Heidi Welch

---

176. According to the agreement, what did Mr. Klein do on October 29?
   (A) He borrowed a vehicle from Ms. Welch.
   (B) He made a deposit at a local bank branch.
   (C) He agreed to rent out a parking space.
   (D) He distributed some parking permits.

177. What information is NOT included in the agreement?
   (A) The date it was signed
   (B) The responsibilities of an owner
   (C) The location of a parking lot
   (D) The role of a parking attendant

178. What is one purpose of the letter?
   (A) To request information
   (B) To accept a job offer
   (C) To end an agreement
   (D) To explain a resignation

179. What does Ms. Welch want Mr. Klein to send?
   (A) An agreement
   (B) A job description
   (C) A receipt
   (D) A deposit

180. Why does Ms. Welch thank Mr. Klein?
   (A) He removed snow from her car.
   (B) He told her about a job.
   (C) A receipt was sent on time.
   (D) An area is always bright at night.

Questions 181–185 refer to the following memo and report.

To: All Factory Personnel
Date: April 8
Subject: Factory Checks

On May 12, the Health Department will carry out an inspection of the factory. This will involve a thorough evaluation of our procedures, storage areas, and food processing machinery. The inspection will get underway at 10:00 A.M. and will be completed by around 12:30 P.M.

Beginning next week, supervisor Kylie Henderson will be checking each section of the factory to identify any machinery that will have to be repaired before May 12.

Please note that she will also be observing employees to make sure they are following these standard procedures:

- cleaning all surfaces in contact with food;
- storing cleaners in the appropriate places;
- wearing protective clothing as required; and
- reporting any problems with equipment to supervisors.

Any questions you have regarding the inspection or Ms. Henderson's assessment should be directed to your supervisor. Thank you for your cooperation.

Claude Keegan
Quality Control Manager
Bistros Biscuits, Ltd.

Results of Pre-Inspection Check

ASSESSMENT PERIOD: April 14 to April 23
OBSERVER: Kylie Henderson

SUMMARY

All areas of the facility and procedures were observed over a ten-day period, during which the observer identified a total of three problems requiring immediate corrective action:

  I. A component on a dough mixer was broken. This had been known to some workers, but because the machine was still able to function satisfactorily, no one notified a supervisor about the problem.

  II. A countertop was not sanitized after use.

  III. An employee was not wearing protective gloves near the ovens.

This report details these findings and provides guidance for avoiding these problems.

– Page 1 –

---

181. What is the purpose of the memo?
(A) To clarify a new procedure
(B) To recommend some changes
(C) To describe some results
(D) To share the details of a plan

182. Who should employees contact if they have a question about the inspection?
(A) An inspector
(B) A Health Department official
(C) Their supervisor
(D) The quality control manager

183. Why was the report created?
(A) To alert employees about some problems
(B) To assist inspectors in their work
(C) To compare several different methods
(D) To report on the progress of a project

184. What can be inferred about the mixer?
(A) It was not checked by Ms. Henderson.
(B) It has to be replaced immediately.
(C) It will be repaired before May 12.
(D) It has not been used since March.

185. Which standard procedure is NOT mentioned in the report?
(A) Cleaning surfaces
(B) Storing cleaners properly
(C) Wearing protective clothing
(D) Reporting equipment problems

GO ON TO THE NEXT PAGE

Questions 186–190 refer to the following Web page, advertisement, and e-mail.

http://www.rexstuxedos.com

Rex's Tuxedo Rentals

| Home | Tuxedos | Accessories | Fitting | About |

Rex's offers contemporary and traditional tuxedos to suit every style. And we are excited to announce that the hottest new styles of tuxedos have been introduced to our rental lineup!

Domino Dayton
- A comfortable tuxedo with a shiny, eye-catching jacket

Antigua Dream
- A great choice for any formal occasion and our only tuxedo in light blue

Panther Padfield
- A classy tuxedo designed by Sal Duval to make you feel like a celebrity

Burgundy Brawn
- A soft blend of wool and cashmere and an all-around fun tuxedo

For more information about these new fashions and our other tuxedos, click here.

Rex's Tuxedo Rentals

Need a tuxedo for a wedding, formal dinner, prom, or red carpet event? Find the latest tuxedo fashions and accessories at Rex's Tuxedo Rentals. We offer unbeatable prices, personal service, and onsite alterations. Plus, we give discounts to customers who rent four or more tuxedos at once…

- Rent 4 tuxedos and get 10% off!
- Rent 5 to 7 tuxedos and get 15% off!
- Rent 8 to 10 tuxedos and get 20% off!
- Rent 11 or more tuxedos and get 25% off!

Got a question? Call us at 555-7545 or come by our shop. We're at 418 Wilshire Boulevard.

From:	Richard Hicks
To:	Don Lawrence
Re:	Tux Rentals
Date:	April 2

Hello Don,

I hope you enjoyed the awards dinner last night. Although the technical award went to another group of engineers, the fact that we were nominated is an honor in itself. Moreover, the software we created has gained recognition as a result of the nomination, which will be good for sales.

If you visit the Web site for the event, you can see a photo of us seated at the table. We must have caught the photographer's attention because the tablecloths were the same shade of light blue that we were wearing.

Today, I have to bring the tuxedos I rented for the team back to Rex's Tuxedo Rentals. John, Barry, and Leroy brought theirs to my apartment. Ryan and Ted left theirs at the office, so I'll pick those up on my way to Rex's. I also want to stop by your place for the one you wore, so I can return all seven together.

Please let me know if you are going to be home at around four o'clock.

Thank you,

Richard

---

186. What has Rex's Tuxedo Rentals announced?
   (A) It has new types of outfits.
   (B) Its location has changed.
   (C) Its opening hours were reduced.
   (D) It has hired a new tailor.

187. What is indicated about the staff at Rex's Tuxedo Rentals?
   (A) They can make adjustments to clothes.
   (B) They provide wedding planning services.
   (C) They were nominated for an award.
   (D) They recently designed some new tuxedos.

188. What type of tuxedo did Mr. Hicks wear to the event?
   (A) Domino Dayton
   (B) Antigua Dream
   (C) Panther Padfield
   (D) Burgundy Brawn

189. What is implied in the e-mail?
   (A) Mr. Lawrence has returned a suit already.
   (B) Mr. Lawrence is Mr. Hicks' supervisor.
   (C) Mr. Hicks and his colleagues developed some software.
   (D) Mr. Hicks' office is beside Rex's Tuxedo Rentals.

190. What discount did Mr. Hicks probably receive?
   (A) 10 percent
   (B) 15 percent
   (C) 20 percent
   (D) 25 percent

GO ON TO THE NEXT PAGE

Questions 191–195 refer to the following e-mail, brochure, and online review.

To:	Heather Clark
From:	Andrew McLean
Date:	Monday, October 3
Re:	Brochure Project

Hello Heather,

Management has just announced that we are recalling one of our microwave ovens. This means we will have to take the information about the item out of the new brochure you are designing, I'm sorry to say. After that, you will have to spread out the other three descriptions and pictures evenly.

Can you take care of page 6 by the end of today? Ideally, we will be able to send the data to the printer tomorrow morning as scheduled.

Best regards,

Andrew
Marketing Department
Olynos Electric

New from Olynos Electric!

Micraway 8000
This versatile microwave makes cooking super convenient. Functioning as an oven and a grill, the Micraway 8000 gives you many cooking options.

Silver Gallance
Olynos Electric's new microwave has twelve heat options, giving the user more control over cooking and reheating items. Powerful but compact, the Silver Gallance is perfect for the smaller kitchen.

Darico Countertop
With more power, this speedy microwave is great for anyone who always has to eat and run. Its stainless steel exterior and spacious interior makes it easy to clean, and it looks great in any kitchen or café.

Zestbox 6000
Designed to make baking breads and cakes easy, the Zestbox's four fans circulate heat to cook or bake food all the way through. This is Olynos Electric's tallest microwave oven with convection capability.

— Page 6 —

https://www.gadgetlovers/olynoselectric/microwaveovens/reviews

November 30

Olynos Electric's Silver Gallance is outstanding. I've been using it for only a few weeks, but now I don't know what I'd do without it! Although it's too small for making loaves of bread, eight dinner rolls fit nicely inside. What's more, I can use it to make all sorts of meals thanks to its many settings. Plus, it doesn't take up much space in my kitchen. A couple months ago, I bought a new Olynos Electric microwave made for baking, and it was useful, too. When it was recalled, I was disappointed, though the replacement I received is just as good or better. If you want a great microwave oven, then get one from Olynos Electric.

Stephanie Bauer

191. What is mentioned about Olynos Electric?
(A) One of its products has been recalled.
(B) Some of its employees design kitchens.
(C) It plans to purchase a new printer.
(D) It has announced the opening of a new factory.

192. Which product has been recalled?
(A) The Micraway 8000
(B) The Silver Gallance
(C) The Darico Countertop
(D) The Zestbox 6000

193. How is the Darico Countertop microwave oven described?
(A) It is attractive.
(B) It is heavy.
(C) It is tall.
(D) It is compact.

194. In the online review, the word "outstanding" in paragraph 1, line 1, is closest in meaning to
(A) excellent
(B) unfinished
(C) durable
(D) tall

195. What is implied in the online review?
(A) Ms. Bauer does not recommend buying Olynos Electric products.
(B) Ms. Bauer is disappointed with her new microwave oven.
(C) The Silver Gallance microwave oven is no longer manufactured.
(D) Olynos Electric replaced Ms. Bauer's microwave oven.

GO ON TO THE NEXT PAGE

Questions 196–200 refer to the following list, schedule, and e-mail.

Albums by Harris Cassidy

Howling Blue Nights
Unlike his first three blues albums, this latest one by Cassidy includes both blues and jazz. It is arguably his most creative recording and brings together many instruments and styles.

Pond Springs Magic
Featuring the popular song "Dreams on the Breeze" and Burney McRae on the saxophone, this blues album consists of songs with strong rhythms and entertaining lyrics.

Mississippi Amber Moon
Cassidy's best-selling album to date, *Mississippi Amber Moon* is a superb collection of blues songs and includes Cassidy's biggest hit ever, "Soul Long."

Songs for the Deluge
The debut album that made Harris Cassidy famous for his outstanding talent on the guitar, *Songs for the Deluge* is now a classic that every blues fan should own.

---

http://www.brookhavenfestival.org

BROOKHAVEN BLUES & JAZZ FESTIVAL

| ABOUT | SCHEDULE | TICKETS | NEWS | VOLUNTEER | CONTACT |

Day One (Saturday, July 19)

Legendary Sheepdogs   2:00–3:40 P.M.
When you combine the mesmerizing voice of Lucille Williams with Gus Reed on the trumpet, you get an exciting yet soothing blend of modern blues. This Alabama band will kick off both days of the festival.

Harris Cassidy   4:00–5:20 P.M.
Considered one of the most talented blues guitarists of all time, Harris Cassidy will play songs from his latest album and of course all of his best-known tunes from the past. This will be an amazing performance, so don't miss it!

The Rusty Nails   5:45–7:10 P.M.
Formed twenty-four years ago, The Rusty Nails have released eleven albums. Known for putting on exciting shows, the band is a must-see for any blues lover. Grab some food at a food stall and enjoy the music!

Daddy Dwyer and the Kings   7:30–9:00 P.M.
If you haven't seen Daddy Dwyer and his band perform, then be ready for a musical experience you'll never forget! Daddy Dwyer and the Kings will close the first day of the festival, which will be immediately followed by a special surprise.

E-Mail Message

From:	<stucker@celeritymail.com>
To:	<organizers@brookhavenfestival.org>
Date:	July 20
Subject:	Music Festival

Thank you for organizing such a fun festival yesterday! The performers were as great as the weather. And the fireworks show at the end was a fantastic addition to this year's event. I had a wonderful time. Unfortunately, however, I lost my watch there. I'm positive that it slipped out of my pocket. And that must have happened during the final performance, which was the only time I sat down on the grass.

If I had noticed it was missing sooner, I would have gone to your information tent inside the venue to let your staff know. Now, I am writing this with the hope that it has been found and was handed over to someone at the tent. If it was, please call me at 555-8994.

Best regards,

Steven Tucker

---

196. Which Harris Cassidy album features different types of music?
- (A) *Howling Blue Nights*
- (B) *Pond Springs Magic*
- (C) *Mississippi Amber Moon*
- (D) *Songs for the Deluge*

197. What is probably true about Harris Cassidy's performance at the festival?
- (A) He performed the song "Soul Long."
- (B) Burney McRae performed with him.
- (C) It was the first musical performance.
- (D) It did not end until after 7:10 P.M.

198. What most likely was the special surprise at the festival?
- (A) A fireworks display
- (B) A gift bag
- (C) A special award
- (D) A fifth performer

199. What is the main purpose of the e-mail?
- (A) To ask about some procedures
- (B) To inquire about a lost item
- (C) To express concern about a venue
- (D) To confirm receipt of some information

200. Who was most likely performing when Mr. Tucker was sitting down?
- (A) Legendary Sheepdogs
- (B) Harris Cassidy
- (C) The Rusty Nails
- (D) Daddy Dwyer and the Kings

Stop! This is the end of the test. If you finish before time is called, you may go back to Parts 5, 6, and 7 and check your work.

解答・解説

解答一覧

リスニング				リーディング			
問題番号	解答	問題番号	解答	問題番号	解答	問題番号	解答
1	C	51	D	101	C	151	C
2	D	52	D	102	A	152	D
3	A	53	D	103	C	153	C
4	D	54	C	104	D	154	B
5	B	55	D	105	A	155	B
6	A	56	A	106	B	156	D
7	C	57	B	107	A	157	A
8	B	58	B	108	A	158	C
9	A	59	A	109	C	159	D
10	A	60	C	110	B	160	C
11	B	61	D	111	C	161	A
12	C	62	A	112	D	162	D
13	B	63	C	113	D	163	B
14	C	64	A	114	C	164	B
15	C	65	A	115	B	165	D
16	B	66	A	116	D	166	B
17	C	67	D	117	D	167	C
18	C	68	B	118	C	168	B
19	A	69	D	119	A	169	B
20	C	70	B	120	B	170	C
21	B	71	D	121	B	171	A
22	A	72	A	122	A	172	C
23	B	73	C	123	B	173	A
24	A	74	D	124	B	174	D
25	C	75	B	125	A	175	B
26	A	76	D	126	B	176	C
27	A	77	D	127	C	177	D
28	B	78	D	128	D	178	C
29	B	79	C	129	A	179	D
30	B	80	A	130	D	180	D
31	C	81	B	131	B	181	D
32	D	82	B	132	B	182	C
33	C	83	C	133	D	183	A
34	B	84	D	134	D	184	C
35	C	85	A	135	D	185	B
36	A	86	B	136	C	186	A
37	B	87	A	137	C	187	A
38	B	88	B	138	B	188	B
39	A	89	D	139	A	189	C
40	C	90	A	140	A	190	B
41	C	91	C	141	C	191	A
42	D	92	A	142	B	192	D
43	D	93	C	143	A	193	A
44	B	94	B	144	D	194	A
45	C	95	B	145	A	195	D
46	A	96	B	146	C	196	A
47	B	97	C	147	C	197	A
48	A	98	D	148	B	198	A
49	C	99	A	149	C	199	B
50	C	100	C	150	B	200	D

予想スコア換算表

リスニング		リーディング	
正解数	換算点	正解数	換算点
96–100	495	96–100	495
91–95	490–495	91–95	465–495
86–90	460–495	86–90	440–480
81–85	440–480	81–85	400–460
76–80	400–460	76–80	365–440
71–75	365–440	71–75	335–420
66–70	335–420	66–70	310–395
61–65	310–395	61–65	275–365
56–60	275–365	56–60	245–340
51–55	245–340	51–55	215–310
46–50	215–310	46–50	190–275
41–45	190–275	41–45	165–255
36–40	165–255	36–40	135–225
31–35	135–225	31–35	115–190
30以下	予想不可能	30以下	予想不可能

▶ 予想スコアの出し方

1. リスニングとリーディングのそれぞれの正解数を数える。
2. 換算表で対応する換算点レンジをそれぞれ見つける。
3. リスニングとリーディングの換算点を足した点が予想スコアになる。

注意：この模試の正解数から本番のTOEICでの正確なスコアを予想することは難しいので、予想スコアは、「おそらくこの範囲内のスコアになる」という幅を持たせたスコアレンジで示してあります。

Part 1 解答・解説

1. 🎧 1-2 🇺🇸

▶ 正解 (C)

女性が書類を手に持っているので、(C)が正解。

(A) 彼女は紙の入っている箱を運んでいる。
(B) 彼女は通知を配っている。
(C) 彼女は書類を手に持っている。
(D) 彼女は引き出しからファイルを取り出している。

☐ **hand out** 配る
☐ **notice** 名 通知
☐ **document** 名 書類
☐ **drawer** 名 引き出し

(A) She's carrying a box of paper.
(B) She's handing out a notice.
(C) She's holding a document.
(D) She's taking files from a drawer.

---

2. 🎧 1-3 🇦🇺

▶ 正解 (D)

1人の男性が人前でホワイトボードを指し示しながら話をしているので、(D)が正解。

(A) 彼らはホワイトボードを壁に固定している。
(B) 彼らはショーウインドーの展示を整えている。
(C) 女性の1人がノートを積み重ねている。
(D) 男性の1人がプレゼンを行っている。

☐ **fasten** 動 固定する
☐ **window display** ショーウインドーの展示
☐ **stack** 動 積み重ねる
☐ **conduct** 動 行う

(A) They're fastening a whiteboard to a wall.
(B) They're setting up a window display.
(C) One of the women is stacking notebooks.
(D) One of the men is conducting a presentation.

---

3. 🎧 1-4 🇨🇦

▶ 正解 (A)

男性がフォークリフトを操縦している写真なので、(A)が正解。vehicleは「車両」を示す名詞で、フォークリフトもvehicleに含まれる。

(A) 男性は車両を操縦している。
(B) 男性はトラックに向かって歩いている。
(C) 男性は建物の屋根を構築している。
(D) 男性は倉庫で作業をしている。

☐ **operate** 動 操縦する
☐ **vehicle** 名 車両
☐ **construct** 動 建てる
☐ **warehouse** 名 倉庫

(A) The man's operating a vehicle.
(B) The man's walking toward a truck.
(C) The man's constructing the roof of a building.
(D) The man's working in a warehouse.

Part 1 | 解答・解説

4. 🎧 1-5 🇬🇧

(A) He's closing some windows.
(B) He's opening a cabinet.
(C) He's folding some blankets.
(D) He's packing a suitcase.

▶ **正解 (D)**

男性がスーツケースに荷物を詰めている写真なので、(D)が正解。

(A) 彼はいくつかの窓を閉めている。
(B) 彼はキャビネットを開けている。
(C) 彼は何枚かの毛布をたたんでいる。
(D) 彼はスーツケースに荷物を詰めている。

- □ **fold** 動 たたむ
- □ **pack** 動 （荷物などを）詰める

5. 🎧 1-6 🇦🇺

(A) Chairs have been piled against a fence.
(B) Tables have been arranged outside.
(C) Posters have been put up beside a deck.
(D) Ropes have been tied to some equipment.

▶ **正解 (B)**

複数のテーブルが屋外に並んでいるので、(B)が正解。

(A) 椅子がフェンスに寄せて積み重ねられている。
(B) テーブルが屋外に並べられている。
(C) ポスターがデッキの横に貼られている。
(D) ロープが機器に結びつけてある。

- □ **pile** 動 積み重ねる
- □ **against** 前 に寄せて
- □ **arrange** 動 並べる
- □ **outside** 副 屋外に
- □ **equipment** 名 機器

6. 🎧 1-7 🇺🇸

(A) One of the men is wearing a tie.
(B) The men are exiting a bus.
(C) The men are facing each other.
(D) One of the men is moving some chairs.

▶ **正解 (A)**

ネクタイをした男性が写っているので、(A)が正解。

(A) 男性の1人はネクタイをしている。
(B) 男性たちはバスを降りている。
(C) 男性たちは互いに向かい合っている。
(D) 男性の1人はいくつかの椅子を動かしている。

- □ **wear** 動 身に着けている
- □ **exit** 動 出る
- □ **face** 動 向かい合う

Part 2 解答・解説

7. 🎧 1-9 🇬🇧 🇦🇺

How many seats should we reserve?
(A) At the awards ceremony.
(B) I agree with them, too.
(C) At least twenty.

私たちは、何席予約すべきですか。
(A) 授賞式で。
(B) 私も彼らに同意します。
(C) 少なくとも20です。

▶ **正解 (C)**

問われているのはHow many seats (何席か) なので、席数を示す(C) At least twenty. (少なくとも20です) が適切な応答。

- □ reserve 動 予約する
- □ award 名 賞
- □ ceremony 名 式典

8. 🎧 1-10 🇬🇧 🇨🇦

Why are you taking pictures?
(A) In a couple of weeks.
(B) They're for our new Web site.
(C) Since around eleven o'clock.

なぜ、あなたは写真を撮っているのですか。
(A) 2、3週間後に。
(B) 私たちの新しいウェブサイトのためにです。
(C) 11時頃から。

▶ **正解 (B)**

なぜ写真を撮っているのかが問われているので、その理由を示唆する(B) They're for our new Web site. (私たちの新しいウェブサイトのためにです) が適切。

- □ a couple of ～ 2、3の～、2つの～

9. 🎧 1-11 🇦🇺 🇺🇸

We haven't booked hotel rooms yet.
(A) We'd better do it soon.
(B) I'm sure it's near the airport.
(C) Oh, I enjoyed reading that book.

私たちは、まだホテルの部屋を予約していません。
(A) 私たちはそれをすぐにすべきです。
(B) 間違いなく空港の近くにあります。
(C) ああ、私はその本を読むのを楽しみました。

▶ **正解 (A)**

「まだホテルの部屋を予約していません」ということは、ホテルの部屋を予約すべき状況にあるということなので、(A) We'd better do it soon. (私たちはそれをすぐにすべきです) が適切。

- □ book 動 予約する
- □ had better ～ ～すべきである

10. 🎧 1-12 🇨🇦 🇬🇧

When were the batteries last replaced?
(A) About a month ago.
(B) Because it stopped running.
(C) This will be the last time.

電池が最後に交換されたのはいつですか。
(A) およそ1ヵ月前です。
(B) それが動かなくなったからです。
(C) これが最後になるでしょう。

▶ **正解 (A)**

「電池が交換されたのはいつか」という問いに対して、時期を示す(A) About a month ago. (およそ1ヵ月前です) が適切な応答。

- □ replace 動 交換する
- □ run 動 動く

Part 2 | 解答・解説

11. 🎧 1-13

Has Ms. Sharma accepted your invitation?
(A) It was sent by post.
(B) No, she won't be able to come.
(C) Everyone except for me.

Sharmaさんは、あなたの招待を受け入れましたか。
(A) それは郵送されました。
(B) いいえ、彼女は来られません。
(C) 私を除き全員です。

▶ **正解 (B)**

Sharmaさんが招待を承諾したかが問われているので、断ったことを「来られない」で表した(B)が正解。

- accept 動 受け入れる
- invitation 名 招待
- by post 郵便で

12. 🎧 1-14

What kind of soup would you like to order?
(A) We're boarding now.
(B) Yes, I would like to.
(C) Something spicy.

どの種類のスープを注文なさいますか。
(A) 私たちは今、搭乗中です。
(B) はい、そうしたいです。
(C) スパイスのきいたものを。

▶ **正解 (C)**

スープの好みが問われているので、スープの種類を示す(C) Something spicy.（スパイスのきいたものを）が適切な応答。

- order 動 注文する
- board 動 乗る
- spicy 形 スパイスのきいた

13. 🎧 1-15

When will the construction of the plant be completed?
(A) It's outside of the city.
(B) By the end of the summer.
(C) We've planted half of them.

工場の建設は、いつ完了しますか。
(A) 市の外です。
(B) 夏の終わりまでには。
(C) 私たちは、それらの半分を植えました。

▶ **正解 (B)**

問われているのは建設工事がいつ完了するのかということなので、期限を示した(B) By the end of the summer.（夏の終わりまでには）が適切な応答。

- construction 名 建設、建設工事
- plant 名 工場
- complete 動 完了する
- plant 動 植える

14. 🎧 1-16

Where did the second interview take place?
(A) It was placed by the door.
(B) The day before yesterday.
(C) On the same floor.

2次面接はどこで行われましたか。
(A) それはドアの近くに置かれていました。
(B) 一昨日。
(C) 同じ階で。

▶ **正解 (C)**

2次面接がどこで行われたのかが問われているので、(C) On the same floor.（同じ階で）が適切な応答。

- interview 名 面接
- take place 行われる
- place 動 置く

15. 🎧 1-17 🇺🇸 🇨🇦

Is the bookstore still open?
(A) I made an extra copy.
(B) Here, use my key.
(C) Yes, for another hour.

書店はまだ開いていますか。
(A) 予備のコピーを取りました。
(B) どうぞ、私の鍵を使ってください。
(C) ええ、あと1時間は。

▶ **正解** (C)

「書店はまだ開いていますか」という問いに対して、あと1時間開いていることを示す(C)が適切な応答。

□ **extra** 形 予備の

16. 🎧 1-18 🇬🇧 🇦🇺

Can you tell me where we are on this map?
(A) You can pick up a copy over there.
(B) Here by the south gate.
(C) No, you were wrong.

私たちがこの地図上のどこにいるのか教えてもらえますか。
(A) あそこで1部もらえますよ。
(B) ここの、南門の近くです。
(C) いいえ、あなたは間違っていました。

▶ **正解** (B)

「私たちが地図上のどこにいるのか」という問いに対し、場所を示した(B) Here by the south gate. (ここの、南門の近くです)が適切な応答。

□ **pick up** 受け取る
□ **copy** 名 部、冊

17. 🎧 1-19 🇨🇦 🇬🇧

Who do I submit travel expense forms to?
(A) Thanks for informing us.
(B) Oh, what time does it leave?
(C) The administration department.

出張費の精算書は誰に提出するのですか。
(A) 私たちに知らせてくださりありがとうございます。
(B) ああ、それは何時に出発しますか。
(C) 総務部です。

▶ **正解** (C)

「出張費の精算書は誰に提出するのか」という問いに対しては、提出すべき部署を示した(C) The administration department. (総務部です)が適切。

□ **submit** 動 提出する
□ **travel expense** 出張費
□ **inform** 動 知らせる

18. 🎧 1-20 🇺🇸 🇦🇺

Weren't you going to reorganize the filing cabinet?
(A) Michael is reviewing the file.
(B) We'll be going together.
(C) I was just about to.

ファイリングキャビネットを整理し直すのではなかったのですか。
(A) Michaelはファイルを見直しています。
(B) 私たちは一緒に行く予定です。
(C) ちょうどするところでした。

▶ **正解** (C)

be about to ～は「まさに～するところである」の意味。「ファイリングキャビネットを整理し直すのではなかったのですか」という問いに対して、(C) I was just about to. (ちょうどするところでした)が適切。

□ **reorganize** 動 整理し直す
□ **review** 動 見直す

19. 🎧 1-21

Would you like us to send you our newsletter?
(A) Oh, I'd appreciate that.
(B) In the newspaper.
(C) That's my old address.

あなたに私たちのニュースレターをお送りしましょうか。
(A) ああ、そうしていただけるとありがたいです。
(B) 新聞で。
(C) それは私の前の住所です。

▶ **正解 (A)**

「私たちのニュースレターをお送りしましょうか」という申し出に対して、申し出を受ける(A) Oh, I'd appreciate that. (ああ、そうしていただけるとありがたいです) が適切な応答。

□ appreciate　動 感謝する

20. 🎧 1-22

When is your appointment at the eye clinic?
(A) It's on Washington Street.
(B) A new director will be appointed soon.
(C) It was yesterday afternoon.

あなたの眼科の予約はいつですか。
(A) Washington Streetにあります。
(B) 新しい部長がもうすぐ任命されます。
(C) 昨日の午後でした。

▶ **正解 (C)**

「あなたの眼科の予約はいつですか」という問いに対して、実は昨日だったことを伝える(C) It was yesterday afternoon. (昨日の午後でした) が適切な応答。

□ appointment　名 予約
□ eye clinic　眼科
□ director　名 部長、取締役
□ appoint　動 任命する

21. 🎧 1-23

We can go over these contracts tomorrow, can't we?
(A) Yes, over on the counter.
(B) I'd rather do it now.
(C) I'm sorry, but I haven't.

私たちは、これらの契約書を明日確認するということでよろしいですね。
(A) ええ、向こうのカウンターの上に。
(B) 私はできれば今したいです。
(C) 申し訳ありませんが、まだしていません。

▶ **正解 (B)**

「契約書を確認するのは明日でよいか」という問いに対して、(B) I'd rather do it now. (私はできれば今したいです) が適切な応答。

□ go over　確認する
□ would rather ~　むしろ~したい

22. 🎧 1-24

Why don't you come here an hour earlier tomorrow?
(A) OK, see you at seven.
(B) Because it was raining.
(C) By the end of the day.

明日、1時間早くここに来てはどうですか。
(A) いいですよ、7時に会いましょう。
(B) 雨が降っていたからです。
(C) 今日中には。

▶ **正解 (A)**

Why don't you ~?は、「~してはどうですか」と人に提案する表現。「明日、1時間早くここに来てはどうですか」に対して、同意を意味する(A) OK, see you at seven. (いいですよ、7時に会いましょう) が適切な応答。

23. 🎧 1-25

Where will you be meeting with them?
(A) Wednesday of last week.
(B) In the hotel lobby.
(C) To discuss our new strategy.

どこで彼らと会う予定ですか。
(A) 先週の水曜日。
(B) ホテルのロビーで。
(C) 私たちの新しい戦略を話し合うために。

▶ 正解 (B)

「どこで彼らと会う予定ですか」には、会う場所を述べた (B) In the hotel lobby.（ホテルのロビーで）が適切な応答。

- ☐ discuss　動 話し合う
- ☐ strategy　名 戦略

24. 🎧 1-26

Do you offer any gardening workshops on weekdays?
(A) Not in September.
(B) Yes, we'll provide the supplies.
(C) Well, it's working right now.

平日に園芸のワークショップを行っていますか。
(A) 9月には行っていません。
(B) はい、私たちは備品を供給します。
(C) ええと、それは現在、動いています。

▶ 正解 (A)

園芸のワークショップが平日に行われているかが問われているので、9月には行われていないことを示す (A) が適切。

- ☐ offer　動 提供する
- ☐ provide　動 供給する
- ☐ supply　名 備品

25. 🎧 1-27

Who will be the keynote speaker at the awards ceremony?
(A) No, the first one.
(B) That speaker is damaged.
(C) I heard that Lucy Martins will be.

授賞式での基調演説者は誰になりますか。
(A) いいえ、最初のものです。
(B) そのスピーカーは壊れています。
(C) 私は Lucy Martins になると聞きました。

▶ 正解 (C)

授賞式での基調演説者が問われているので、(C) I heard that Lucy Martins will be.（私は Lucy Martins になると聞きました）が適切。

- ☐ keynote speaker　基調演説者
- ☐ award　名 賞
- ☐ damaged　形 壊れた、損傷を受けた

26. 🎧 1-28

What size apartment is he looking to rent?
(A) One with two bedrooms.
(B) A different building.
(C) Yes, and they looked fine.

彼はどの広さのアパートを探していますか。
(A) 寝室が2つある物件を。
(B) 別の建物です。
(C) ええ、そしてそれらはよさそうに見えました。

▶ 正解 (A)

彼が探しているアパートの広さが問われているので、(A) One with two bedrooms.（寝室が2つある物件を）が適切な応答。寝室の数がアパートの広さを示している。

- ☐ rent　動 賃借する

27.

Will Claudia be applying for the position at the overseas branch office?
(A) She decided not to.
(B) The supervisor.
(C) I heard she's arriving today.

Claudiaは、海外支社での職に応募するのでしょうか。
(A) 彼女はそうしないことに決めました。
(B) 上司です。
(C) 彼女は今日到着すると聞きました。

▶ 正解 (A)

「Claudiaは、海外支社での職に応募するのでしょうか」には、彼女の意向を示した(A) She decided not to. (彼女はそうしないことに決めました) が適切な応答。

- apply for ~　~に応募する
- position　名 職
- overseas　形 海外の
- branch　名 支社、支店
- decide　動 決める

28.

You'd better contact the payroll department about the change of address.
(A) Please address the package to me.
(B) I've already let them know.
(C) About forty-five minutes ago.

住所の変更について、給与課に連絡すべきです。
(A) 小包を私宛てにしてください。
(B) すでに知らせました。
(C) およそ45分前です。

▶ 正解 (B)

給与課に連絡すべきであるという指摘には、(B) I've already let them know. (すでに知らせました) が適切な応答。

- had better ~　~すべきである
- contact　動 連絡する
- payroll　名 給与事務
- department　名 部署、課
- address A to B　AをB宛てにする

29.

Would you like this fan on, or shall I turn it off?
(A) Yeah, he's off today.
(B) Leave it on, please.
(C) I'll have one of those.

この扇風機はつけておきましょうか、それとも切りましょうか。
(A) ええ、彼は今日休みです。
(B) つけたままにしておいてください。
(C) 私はそれらの1つをいただきます。

▶ 正解 (B)

Would you like this fan onのonは機械や電化製品などが作動している状態を示す形容詞。「扇風機はつけておくのがいいか、切った方がいいか」という問いなので、(B) Leave it on, please. (つけたままにしておいてください) が適切な応答。

- turn off　~を切る、消す
- leave　動 そのままの状態にしておく

30.

Are you going to correct the error in the press release?
(A) Actually, that was a mistake.
(B) Jessica is taking care of that.
(C) Some donations were collected.

あなたはプレスリリースの誤りを訂正しますか。
(A) 実は、それは間違いでした。
(B) Jessicaが対応しています。
(C) いくらかの寄付金が集められました。

▶ 正解 (B)

「あなたは誤りを訂正しますか」という問いには、(B) Jessica is taking care of that. (Jessicaが対応しています) が適切な応答。

- correct　動 訂正する
- take care of ~　~に対応する
- donation　名 寄付金
- collect　動 集める

31.

Should we schedule the press conference for the morning or the afternoon?
(A) They're both on time.
(B) They completely agreed.
(C) I prefer the morning.

私たちは記者会見を午前に入れるべきですか、それとも午後にしましょうか。
(A) 共に時間通りです。
(B) 彼らは完全に同意しました。
(C) 私は午前のほうがいいです。

▶ 正解 (C)

記者会見を午前にするか、午後にするかが問われているので、(C) I prefer the morning.（私は午前のほうがいいです）が適切。

- schedule 動 予定に入れる
- press conference 記者会見
- on time 時間通り
- completely 副 完全に

Part 3 解答・解説

Questions 32 through 34 refer to the following conversation.

問題32〜34は次の会話に関するものです。

M: Excuse me. I don't suppose you sell work boots here, do you? It looks as though you have only sneakers and formal footwear.

W: No—sorry—we don't carry them. We should, though. Since the construction started on the stadium, quite a few people have asked me if we have those. I tell them to go to the big hardware store in the shopping mall.

M: All right, I'll head over there next. And thanks for your help. I'm going to be working at the stadium myself, and the job starts tomorrow, so I hope to find a pair soon.

男性：すみません。ここには作業用ブーツは売っていませんよね。スニーカーとフォーマルな靴しかないようですが。

女性：いいえ、申し訳ございません、当店では取り扱っておりません。本当は置くべきですが。スタジアムの建設工事が始まって以来、かなりの数のお客様が作業用ブーツはあるかとお尋ねになっています。ショッピングモールの大きなホームセンターに行くようにお伝えしています。

男性：わかりました、次はそこに行きます。ありがとうございます。私自身もスタジアムで働くことになっていて、明日から仕事が始まるので、早く一足見つけたいと思っています。

- suppose 動 〜と思う
- I don't suppose 〜 〜ではないですよね（質問や依頼をする時に用いる丁寧な表現）
- as though 〜 〜であるかのように
- carry 動 （店が商品として）取り扱う
- construction 名 建設工事
- quite a few かなりの数の
- hardware store ホームセンター
- head 動 向かう

32.

Where most likely does the woman work?
(A) At a construction site
(B) At a hardware store
(C) At a shopping mall
(D) At a shoe store

女性はおそらくどこで働いていますか。
(A) 建設現場
(B) ホームセンター
(C) ショッピングモール
(D) 靴屋

▶ **正解** (D)

男性の It looks as though you have only sneakers and formal footwear.（スニーカーとフォーマルな靴しかないようですが）から、女性が働いているのは、靴屋であると推測できる。

33.

What does the man want to know?
(A) If a stadium will open soon
(B) If some hardware is required
(C) If a type of product is available
(D) If an event has already started

男性は何を知りたいですか。
(A) スタジアムがもうじきオープンするかどうか
(B) 工具が必要かどうか
(C) ある種の商品があるかどうか
(D) イベントがすでに開始したかどうか

▶ **正解** (C)

男性は女性に I don't suppose you sell work boots here, do you?（ここには作業用ブーツは売っていませんよね）と尋ねているので、work boots（作業用ブーツ）を a type of product（ある種の商品）で言い換えた(C)が正解。

□ require　動 必要とする
□ available　形 入手できる

34.

What does the man say he will do tomorrow?
(A) Visit a nearby business
(B) Start a new job
(C) Submit an application form
(D) Buy a uniform

男性は明日何をすると言っていますか。
(A) 近くの店に行く
(B) 新しい仕事を始める
(C) 応募書類を提出する
(D) 制服を買う

▶ **正解** (B)

男性は、I'm going to be working at the stadium myself, and the job starts tomorrow（私自身もスタジアムで働くことになっていて、明日から仕事が始まる）と言っているので、(B)が正解。(A)は明日ではなく、この後すぐにやることなので不正解。

□ nearby　形 近くの
□ submit　動 提出する
□ application　名 応募

▶ **言い換えポイント**　the job starts tomorrow ➡ Start a new job

🎧 1-36

Questions 35 through 37 refer to the following conversation with three speakers.

W-A: We're ready to open tomorrow. The opening ceremony will be outside the dealership at two o'clock.

W-B: I called the catering company and placed an order. They'll bring the food at 1:30 tomorrow afternoon.

M: About thirty people will be here. I'm worried that there are too many cars in the front lot. There might not be enough space.

W-B: We should move some cars. We could park them in the back lot.

M: I agree. We don't want a group of people standing around the cars we hope to sell— one might get a scratch.

W-A: OK, I can move some of them tomorrow morning.

問題35〜37は3人の話し手による次の会話に関するものです。

女性A：明日のオープンの準備は出来ています。開業式は、販売店の外で2時から行われます。

女性B：ケータリング会社に電話して、注文しておきました。彼らは明日の午後1時30分に食べ物を届けてくれます。

男性　：およそ30人が来る予定です。表の駐車場に車が多すぎるのが心配です。十分なスペースがないかもしれません。

女性B：車を何台か移動するべきです。裏の駐車場に置けるでしょう。

男性　：賛成です。売ろうと思っている車の周りにかたまって立っていてほしくありません。車にひっかき傷がつくかもしれませんし。

女性A：わかりました、明日の朝、私が何台か移動しましょう。

- **dealership** 名 販売代理店（特に自動車販売店を表すことが多い）
- **place an order** 注文をする
- **lot** 名 駐車場
- **scratch** 名 ひっかき傷

35.

What type of business are the speakers planning to open?
(A) A parking garage
(B) A catering company
(C) A car dealership
(D) A grocery store

話し手は、どんな業種の会社を開業する予定ですか。
(A) 駐車場ビル
(B) ケータリング会社
(C) 自動車販売店
(D) 食料品店

▶ 正解　(C)

冒頭の We're ready to open tomorrow. The opening ceremony will be outside the dealership at two o'clock.（明日のオープンの準備は出来ています。開業式は、販売店の外で2時から行われます）から販売店がオープンすることがわかる。また、後半の the cars we hope to sell（売ろうと思っている車）から、車を商品として販売することがわかる。よって、(C)が正解。

- **parking garage** 駐車場ビル
- **grocery store** 食料品店、スーパー

36.

Why is the man concerned?
(A) An area might be too small.
(B) A sale might be finished.
(C) A customer might be late.
(D) A business might be closed.

男性はなぜ心配していますか。
(A) 場所が狭すぎるかもしれない。
(B) セールが終わっているかもしれない。
(C) 顧客が遅れるかもしれない。
(D) 店が閉まっているかもしれない。

▶ 正解　(A)

男性のI'm worried that there are too many cars in the front lot. There might not be enough space.（表の駐車場に車が多すぎるのが心配です。十分なスペースがないかもしれません）から、男性は十分な場所がないことを懸念していることがわかるので、(A)が正解。

- concerned　形 心配している
- finished　形 終わっている
- closed　形 閉まっている

▶ 言い換えポイント　not enough space ➡ too small

37.

What does one of the women offer to do?
(A) Send some cards
(B) Move some cars
(C) Place some orders
(D) Buy some food

女性の1人は、何をすると申し出ていますか。
(A) カードを送る
(B) 車を移動する
(C) 注文を出す
(D) 食料を買う

▶ 正解　(B)

女性AのI can move some of them tomorrow morning.（明日の朝、私が何台か移動しましょう）におけるthemは、前文のcars（車）を指している。翌朝に車を動かすことを申し出ているので、(B)が正解。

🎧 1-37

Questions 38 through 40 refer to the following conversation.

W: I'm sorry to interrupt, but does anyone know where the projector is? I need it for my presentation, which starts in fifteen minutes.

M: It's not in the cabinet in the conference room? That's where I saw it last—on Friday.

W: I've already looked in there, and I didn't see it in the storeroom, either.

M: Wait, then you should give Cindy a call. She's working in a different department today, but yesterday she was here until six training the new data analysts. She can probably tell you where it is.

問題38〜40は次の会話に関するものです。

女性：すみませんが、どなたかプロジェクターがどこにあるか知りませんか。15分後に始まるプレゼンに必要です。

男性：会議室のキャビネットの中にありませんか。私が最後に見たのはそこです。金曜日にです。

女性：そこはすでに見ましたし、倉庫でも見つかりませんでした。

男性：ちょっと待って、それならCindyに電話をするべきです。彼女は今日、別の部署で勤務していますが、昨日は6時までここで新しいデータアナリストの研修をしていました。きっと彼女はプロジェクターがどこにあるのか教えてくれるでしょう。

□ **interrupt** 動 邪魔をする　□ **conference room** 会議室　□ **storeroom** 名 倉庫、物置
□ **department** 名 部署　□ **train** 動 研修をする　□ **analyst** 名 分析者、アナリスト
□ **probably** 副 おそらく

38.

What has the woman been looking for?
(A) A room
(B) A device
(C) A coworker
(D) A record

女性は何を探していますか。
(A) 部屋
(B) 機器
(C) 同僚
(D) 記録

▶ 正解 (B)

女性は、does anyone know where the projector is?（どなたかプロジェクターがどこにあるか知りませんか）と言っているので、プロジェクターを探していることがわかる。プロジェクターはdevice（機器）であるから、(B)が正解。

□ **coworker** 名 同僚

▶ 言い換えポイント　the projector ➡ A device

64

39.

What does the woman tell the man?
(A) She checked two rooms.
(B) She had a technical problem.
(C) She looked for an item in a store.
(D) She could not present a report.

女性は、男性に何を伝えていますか。
(A) 2つの部屋を調べた。
(B) 技術的な問題があった。
(C) 店で品物を探した。
(D) 報告のプレゼンができなかった。

▶ 正解 (A)

男性のIt's not in the cabinet in the conference room? (会議室のキャビネットの中にありませんか) に対する女性の I've already looked in there, and I didn't see it in the storeroom, either. (そこはすでに見ましたし、倉庫でも見つかりませんでした) から、女性が会議室と倉庫の両方を見たことがわかるので、(A)が正解。

- □ technical 形 技術上の
- □ present 動 プレゼンをする

40.

What does the man suggest the woman do?
(A) Attend a presentation
(B) Postpone a project
(C) Contact a coworker
(D) Review some data

男性は、女性に何をするよう提案していますか。
(A) プレゼンに出席する
(B) プロジェクトを延期する
(C) 同僚に連絡する
(D) データを見直す

▶ 正解 (C)

男性は、Wait, then you should give Cindy a call. (ちょっと待って、それならCindyに電話をするべきです) と言っているので、(C) が正解。

▶ 言い換えポイント　give Cindy a call ➡ Contact a coworker

- □ attend 動 出席する
- □ postpone 動 延期する
- □ contact 動 連絡を取る
- □ review 動 見直す

🎧 1-38

Questions 41 through 43 refer to the following conversation.

M: Sherri, I heard that you've been to the Reno Social Media Conference. How was it? I'm considering going.

W: You really should. At the time I went—a few years ago—I was helping design our company's blog. The conference workshops provided me with a great deal of practical information I could use for that project.

M: Oh, you worked on that? I didn't know. I've been put in charge of assembling a team for a new social media project. We'll probably organize a photography contest. Are you interested in working with us on that?

W: Very much so! As for the conference, I'm sure there'll be plenty of chances to learn about photography in marketing.

問題41〜43は次の会話に関するものです。

男性：Sherri、あなたはReno Social Media Conferenceに参加したことがあるそうですね。どうでしたか。私も参加しようかと考えています。

女性：ぜひ参加すべきです。私が行ったのは2、3年前になりますが、その当時、私は会社のブログをデザインすることを手伝っていました。会議ワークショップは、そのプロジェクトで私が使うことのできた多くの実践的な情報を与えてくれました。

男性：ああ、あなたはあれを手がけていたのですか。知りませんでした。私は、新しいソーシャルメディアプロジェクトのチームを立ち上げる任務を与えられました。おそらく写真コンテストを企画することになります。私たちと一緒にそれをやることに興味がありますか。

女性：とてもあります。会議のことですが、マーケティングの写真に関して学べるチャンスがきっとたくさんありますよ。

- □ provide 動 与える　□ a great deal of 〜 多くの〜　□ practical 形 実践的な
- □ work on 取り組む　□ in charge of 〜 〜の担当　□ assemble 動 (人を)集める
- □ photography 名 写真　□ plenty of 〜 たくさんの〜

41.

Why does the man talk to the woman?
(A) To offer some assistance
(B) To discuss a research project
(C) To find out about a conference
(D) To register for some workshops

男性はなぜ女性に話しかけていますか。
(A) 援助を申し出るため
(B) 研究プロジェクトについて話し合うため
(C) 会議について情報を得るため
(D) ワークショップに登録するため

▶ 正解 (C)

男性は、Sherri, I heard that you've been to the Reno Social Media Conference. How was it? (Sherri、あなたはReno Social Media Conferenceに参加したことがあるそうですね。どうでしたか) と尋ねている。会議について尋ねているので、(C)が正解。

- □ offer 動 申し出る
- □ assistance 名 援助
- □ discuss 動 話し合う
- □ research 名 研究
- □ find out about 〜 〜について情報を得る
- □ register 動 登録する

66

42.

What does the woman suggest the man do?
(A) Read a blog
(B) Verify some information
(C) Change a design
(D) Attend a conference

女性は男性に何をするように勧めていますか。
(A) ブログを読む
(B) 情報を確かめる
(C) デザインを変更する
(D) 会議に出席する

▶ 正解 (D)

男性のI'm considering going.（私も参加しようかと考えています）に対し女性は、You really should.（ぜひ参加すべきです）と言っている。the Reno Social Media Conferenceについて話しているので、(D)が正解。

□ **verify** 動 確かめる
□ **attend** 動 出席する

43.

What is the woman interested in doing?
(A) Taking photographs
(B) Designing a blog
(C) Entering a contest
(D) Joining a project

女性は、何をすることに興味がありますか。
(A) 写真を撮ること
(B) ブログをデザインすること
(C) コンテストに参加すること
(D) プロジェクトに加わること

▶ 正解 (D)

男性のAre you interested in working with us on that?（私たちと一緒にそれをやることに興味がありますか）に対し女性は、Very much so!（とてもあります）と言っている。男性の質問にあるthatは、その前のa new social media project（新しいソーシャルメディアプロジェクト）を指しているので、(D)が正解。

□ **enter** 動 参加する
□ **join** 動 加わる

🎧 1-39

Questions 44 through 46 refer to the following conversation.

M: *Northfolk Tribune* Subscription Department.

W: Hi, my name is Fiona Tipton. I live at 22 Kirkwood Avenue, and I'm calling because I haven't received my paper. I suspended my subscription before a business trip two weeks ago. I used your online form to do that. Could I have cancelled it by mistake?

M: No, we have a different form for cancellations, so it must be something else. Let me check your subscription status… OK, it looks as if you selected the seventeenth as the date to resume delivery. That's tomorrow, but we'll bring you one today if you want.

W: Oh, I thought I'd selected the eleventh. Yes, please send today's. And thanks for your help!

問題44〜46は次の会話に関するものです。

男性：*Northfolk Tribune* の購読部でございます。

女性：もしもし、私の名前はFiona Tiptonです。住所は22 Kirkwood Avenueで、新聞を受け取っていないので電話をしています。2週間前、出張に行く前に購読を一時的に止めました。そちらのオンラインのフォームを使ったのですが。間違って購読を解約してしまったのでしょうか。

男性：いいえ、解約には別のフォームがありますので、何か別の理由があるはずです。購読状況をお調べいたします。わかりました。どうやら配達を再開する日付を17日になさったようですね。それは明日ですが、ご希望でしたら本日1部お届けいたします。

女性：ああ、11日にしたと思っていました。ええ、今日のものを届けてください。助かります。

- □ **suspend** 動 一時的に止める □ **subscription** 名 購読 □ **cancel** 動 解約する
- □ **by mistake** 間違って □ **cancellation** 名 解約 □ **status** 名 状況 □ **select** 動 選ぶ
- □ **resume** 動 再開する □ **delivery** 名 配達

44.

What is the purpose of the call?
(A) To cancel an appointment
(B) To see if an error was made
(C) To ask if an item was found
(D) To reschedule a delivery

電話の目的は何ですか。
(A) 会う約束をキャンセルすること
(B) 間違いがあったか確認すること
(C) 品物が見つかったか尋ねること
(D) 配達の予定を変更すること

▶ 正解　(B)

女性は、出張に行く前に新聞の配達を一時的に止める手続きをしたが、配達再開日を過ぎても新聞が配達されないので、オンライン上で配達の一時停止の手続きをする際に誤って解約してしまったのではないかと心配している。その確認のために電話をしているので、(B)が正解。

- □ **appointment** 名 会う約束
- □ **reschedule** 動 予定を入れ直す

45.

Why did the woman fill out a form?
(A) To report a change of address
(B) To order some travel accessories
(C) To put a subscription on hold
(D) To book accommodation

女性はなぜフォームに記入しましたか。
(A) 住所の変更を報告するため
(B) 旅行用品を注文するため
(C) 購読を一時的に止めるため
(D) 宿泊施設を予約するため

▶ 正解 (C)

女性は、I suspended my subscription before a business trip two weeks ago. I used your online form to do that. (2週間前、出張に行く前に購読を一時的に止めました。そちらのオンラインのフォームを使ったのですが) と言っているので、(C)が正解。

- report 動 報告する
- put 〜 on hold 〜を一時停止する
- book 動 予約する
- accommodation 名 宿泊施設

▶ 言い換えポイント suspended my subscription
➡ put a subscription on hold

46.

What does the man offer to do today?
(A) Deliver a newspaper
(B) Provide some instructions
(C) Prepare a new form
(D) Accept a submission

男性は今日何をすることを申し出ていますか。
(A) 新聞を届ける
(B) 指示を与える
(C) 新しいフォームを用意する
(D) 提出を受理する

▶ 正解 (A)

男性の we'll bring you one today if you want. (ご希望でしたら本日1部お届けいたします) における one は新聞を指しているので、(A)のように言い換えることができる。

- provide 動 与える
- instructions 名 (複数形で) 指示
- prepare 動 用意する
- accept 動 受理する
- submission 名 提出

▶ 言い換えポイント bring you one ➡ Deliver a newspaper

Questions 47 through 49 refer to the following conversation.

問題47〜49は次の会話に関するものです。

W: Hi. I just received an e-mail from you confirming my booking in September. But I must have made an error on your online form. I'd like two rooms, not one.

女性：もしもし。たった今そちらから、9月の予約の確認のメールを受け取りました。でも、私はそちらのオンラインフォーム上で間違えたに違いありません。1部屋ではなく、2部屋希望します。

M: OK, could you tell me your name, please? I'll check your reservation and whether a room is available on that date.

男性：わかりました。お名前を頂けますか。ご予約を確認して、その日に1部屋空きがあるかお調べいたします。

W: Sure. It's Janice Wallis. W-A-L-L-I-S. Oh, would you also let me know the total for both rooms? My coworker and I will be in town on business, and I'm trying to figure out how much everything will be.

女性：わかりました。名前はJanice Wallisです。W-A-L-L-I-Sです。ああ、それから両方の部屋の合計金額も教えてもらえますか。同僚と私は仕事でそちらに行くので、全部でいくらになるか計算しようとしています。

M: Of course, ma'am. Another single room is available, and the total for both is $378. If you'd like, I'll reserve it for you now and send you an updated confirmation message.

男性：かしこまりました、お客様。シングルがもう1部屋空いておりまして、両方の合計は378ドルです。ご希望でしたらすぐにご予約いたしまして、更新された確認メッセージをお送りいたします。

- □ confirm 動 確認する
- □ booking 名 予約
- □ reservation 名 予約
- □ whether 接 〜かどうか
- □ coworker 名 同僚
- □ on business 仕事で
- □ figure out 算出する
- □ reserve 動 予約する
- □ updated 形 更新された
- □ confirmation 名 確認

47.

Why is the woman calling?
(A) To confirm a payment
(B) To make an additional reservation
(C) To correct a billing error
(D) To request a form

女性はなぜ電話をかけていますか。
(A) 支払いを確かめるため
(B) 追加の予約をするため
(C) 請求の間違いを訂正するため
(D) 用紙を求めるため

▶ 正解 (B)

女性は、本当は2部屋予約すべきところを誤って、1部屋分の予約しかしなかったことを伝えている。この電話の目的はもう1部屋予約することなので、(B)が正解。

- □ payment 名 支払い
- □ additional 形 追加の
- □ correct 動 訂正する
- □ billing 名 請求
- □ request 動 求める

48.

What does the woman tell the man?
(A) She is trying to calculate a total.
(B) She is arranging to stay with a relative.
(C) She is expecting to arrive on a later date.
(D) She is planning to purchase two books.

女性は、男性に何を伝えていますか。
(A) 合計を計算しようとしている。
(B) 親戚の家に滞在する手配をしている。
(C) 後日到着することを見込んでいる。
(D) 本を2冊購入する予定である。

▶ **正解 (A)**

女性のwould you also let me know the total for both rooms? (両方の部屋の合計金額も教えてもらえますか) や I'm trying to figure out how much everything will be. (全部でいくらになるか計算しようとしています) から、(A)が正解。

- □ calculate 動 計算する
- □ arrange 動 手配する
- □ relative 名 親戚
- □ expect 動 見込む
- □ purchase 動 購入する

▶ 言い換えポイント　figure out how much everything will be
➡ calculate a total

49.

What does the man offer to do?
(A) Provide a registration form
(B) Make a recommendation
(C) Send a message
(D) Refund a deposit

男性は何をすると申し出ていますか。
(A) 登録用紙を配布する
(B) 推薦をする
(C) メッセージを送る
(D) 保証金を払い戻す

▶ **正解 (C)**

男性は、If you'd like, I'll reserve it for you now and send you an updated confirmation message. (ご希望でしたらすぐにご予約いたしまして、更新された確認メッセージをお送りいたします) と言っているので、(C)が正解。

- □ provide 動 提供する、配る
- □ registration 名 登録
- □ recommendation 名 推薦
- □ refund 動 払い戻す
- □ deposit 名 保証金

🎧 1-41

Questions 50 through 52 refer to the following conversation.

問題50〜52は次の会話に関するものです。

W: Hey, Eric! How many copies of this handout do you want me to make for the meeting?

M: Twenty-five should be enough, but hold on—that's not the one I need.

W: Did I take the wrong sheet from your desk?

M: No, I must have printed out the wrong file. I updated that graph to include our sales forecast for next year. If I e-mail the revised version to you, can you print it out?

W: Sure. And the meeting—when's it starting?

M: Now, so I have to get upstairs. Would you mind bringing the copies to me?

W: Not at all. Which floor?

M: Thirty-two. I'll be in the boardroom. Thanks a lot, Sophie!

女性：あの、Eric、会議用にこの配布資料を何部コピーすればいいのですか。

男性：25部で十分ですが、ちょっと待って。それは私が必要としているものとは違います。

女性：あなたの机から違う紙を取ってしまったのでしょうか。

男性：いや、私が間違ったファイルを印刷したに違いありません。来年の販売予測を入れるためにそのグラフを更新しました。改訂版をメールで送ったら、印刷してもらえますか。

女性：いいですよ。それで会議ですが、いつ始まりますか。

男性：今です。ですから私は上の階に行かなければなりません。コピーを持ってきてもらえませんか。

女性：かまいませんよ。何階ですか。

男性：32階です。私は重役用会議室にいます。どうもありがとう、Sophie。

- **handout** 名 配布資料   □ **hold on** 待つ   □ **update** 動 更新する   □ **include** 動 含める
- **forecast** 名 予測   □ **revised version** 改訂版   □ **upstairs** 副 階上へ
- **boardroom** 名 重役用会議室

50.

What does the man want the woman to copy?
(A) A schedule
(B) A floor plan
(C) A handout
(D) A sales contract

男性は、女性に何をコピーしてほしいのですか。
(A) 予定表
(B) 間取図
(C) 配布資料
(D) 売買契約書

▶ 正解 (C)

女性のHow many copies of this handout do you want me to make for the meeting?（会議用にこの配布資料を何部コピーすればいいのですか）から、男性がコピーを求めているのは、(C) A handout（配布資料）であるとわかる。

▶ 言い換えポイント　to make copies ➡ to copy

51.

What is the problem?
(A) A file has been damaged.
(B) A meeting has already ended.
(C) Some paper is the wrong size.
(D) Some information is incomplete.

何が問題ですか。
(A) ファイルが破損している。
(B) 会議はすでに終了した。
(C) 用紙のサイズが間違っている。
(D) 情報が不完全である。

▶ 正解 (D)

男性は、女性がコピーしようとしている配布資料中のグラフが更新前のものであることに気付き、改訂版を印刷するように女性に頼んでいる。更新前のグラフには来年の販売予測が入っていないので、(D)のように言い換えることができる。

☐ damage 動 損傷を与える
☐ end 動 終える
☐ incomplete 形 不完全な

52.

What does the woman agree to do?
(A) Update a document
(B) Make thirty-two copies
(C) Participate in a meeting
(D) Go to another floor

女性は何をすることに同意していますか。
(A) 文書を更新する
(B) 32部のコピーを取る
(C) 会議に参加する
(D) 別の階に行く

▶ 正解 (D)

男性のI have to get upstairs. Would you mind bringing the copies to me? (私は上の階に行かなければなりません。コピーを持ってきてもらえませんか) に対し、女性はNot at all. (かまいませんよ) と答えているので、女性はコピーを上の階へ届けることに同意している。よって、(D)が正解。

Would you mind -ing?
〜してもらえませんか
丁寧な依頼表現。文字通り訳すと「〜するのは嫌ですか」という意味なので、依頼を承諾する時は、Not at all. (それをすることは全く嫌ではない＝かまわない) を用いることが多い。

▶ 言い換えポイント　get upstairs → Go to another floor

🎧 1-42

Questions 53 through 55 refer to the following conversation.

問題53〜55は次の会話に関するものです。

W: You look busy, Bobby—I'm sorry to bother you, but I just noticed that the stack of flyers is still there by the door. Weren't you going to bring them to the mailroom?

M: Right—I'll see to that in a moment. But first, could you show me where we keep the list of former customers? I can't find it in the database.

W: That's because it's not there. The customer information is stored in the mailroom only. It's one way the company safeguards privacy.

M: Oh, OK. So the clerks there will know where to send those advertisements. Thanks, Claudia.

女性：忙しそうですね、Bobby。邪魔をしてすみませんが、チラシの束がまだドアの脇にあるのに気付きました。あなたがそれらを郵便管理室に持って行くことになっていませんでしたか。

男性：その通りです。この後すぐにそれをやります。でもまず、過去の顧客のリストがどこに保管してあるか教えてもらえませんか。データベース中には見つかりません。

女性：それは、そこにはないからです。顧客情報は、郵便管理室にだけ保管してあります。それは、会社がプライバシーを保護する方法の1つです。

男性：ああ、わかりました。では、そこの事務員なら、その広告をどこに送るかわかりますね。ありがとう、Claudia。

☐ bother 動 邪魔をする   ☐ notice 動 気付く   ☐ stack of ~ ~の束   ☐ flyer 名 チラシ
☐ mailroom 名 郵便管理室   ☐ see to ~ ~に対応する   ☐ in a moment すぐに
☐ former 形 前の   ☐ safeguard 動 保護する   ☐ clerk 名 事務員

53.

Why does the woman apologize to the man?
(A) She left the door to the room open.
(B) She believes that she made a mistake.
(C) She has not finished an assignment.
(D) She thinks that she has interrupted him.

女性はなぜ男性に謝っていますか。
(A) 部屋のドアを開けっぱなしにした。
(B) 間違いをしたと思っている。
(C) 任務を終えていない。
(D) 彼の邪魔をしたと思っている。

▶ 正解 (D)

女性のI'm sorry to bother you（邪魔をしてすみません）から、(D)を選ぶ。

▶ 言い換えポイント   bother you ➡ has interrupted him

☐ apologize 動 謝る
☐ assignment 名 （与えられた）任務
☐ interrupt 動 邪魔をする

54.

What does the man mean when he says, "I'll see to that in a moment"?
(A) He will look through some mail.
(B) He will check an advertisement.
(C) He will take away some flyers.
(D) He will post a notice in a room.

男性が "I'll see to that in a moment" と言っているのはどういう意味ですか。
(A) 郵便物に目を通す。
(B) 広告を確認する。
(C) チラシを持って行く。
(D) 部屋に通知を掲示する。

▶ **正解** (C)

男性は、女性にWeren't you going to bring them to the mailroom?(あなたが[チラシを]郵便管理室に持って行くことになっていませんでしたか)と指摘され、I'll see to that in a moment.(この後すぐにそれをやります)と答えている。このthatはチラシを郵便管理室に持って行くことなので、(C)が正解。

□ **look through** 目を通す
□ **take away** 持って行く
□ **post** 動 掲示する
□ **notice** 名 通知

▶ 言い換えポイント　bring them to the mailroom
　→ take away some flyers

55.

According to the woman, how is some information protected?
(A) By restricting access to an area
(B) By regularly changing a password
(C) By having a guard on duty
(D) By keeping it in one place

女性によると、情報はどのように保護されていますか。
(A) ある場所への立ち入りを制限することによって
(B) パスワードを定期的に変更することによって
(C) 警備員を配置することによって
(D) 1カ所に保管することによって

▶ **正解** (D)

女性のThe customer information is stored in the mailroom only. It's one way the company safeguards privacy.(顧客情報は、郵便管理室にだけ保管してあります。それは、会社がプライバシーを保護する方法の1つです)に、この会社の個人情報を守る方法が示されており、それは(D)の内容と一致する。

□ **restrict** 動 制限する
□ **regularly** 副 定期的に
□ **on duty** 勤務している

▶ 言い換えポイント　The customer information is stored in the mailroom
　→ keep it in one place

Questions 56 through 58 refer to the following conversation with three speakers.

問題56〜58は3人の話し手による次の会話に関するものです。

W: Listen up, everyone! A new service technician will start work here tomorrow morning. His name's Gary, and someone will have to show him around.

女性：聞いてください、皆さん。新しい整備士が、明朝からここで働き始めます。彼の名前はGaryで、誰かに彼を案内してもらう必要があるのですが。

M-A: I can do that. What time's he coming in?

男性A：私がやりますよ。彼は何時に来ますか。

W: He'll be here when we open. And thanks, Eddie.

女性：開店時間に来る予定です。ありがとう、Eddie。

M-B: Um, but shouldn't a technician show him where we keep all our tools?

男性B：あの、でも誰か整備士が、全ての道具の場所を教えたほうがよいのではないですか。

M-A: Good point. Why don't you do it?

男性A：なるほど、そうですね。あなたがやってくれますか。

M-B: Well, I've got to finish fixing this braking system for a customer by ten tomorrow. If I can get it done today, I'll give Gary the tour.

男性B：ええと、私は明日の10時までに、このブレーキ装置の修理をお客様のために終えなければなりません。もし今日中に修理を終えられれば、私がGaryを案内しましょう。

W: Thanks, Raymond. And if you need time before ten to complete the work on that car, Gary can wait. Besides, he'll have to do some paperwork first. I'll introduce you to him after he's done in my office.

女性：ありがとう、Raymond。もしその車の作業を終えるのに10時までかかるなら、Garyには待ってもらいます。それに、彼はまず事務手続きをしなければなりませんので。彼が私のオフィスでそれを終えたら、あなたを彼に紹介しましょう。

☐ service technician 整備士　☐ tour 名 案内　☐ complete 動 完了する
☐ paperwork 名 事務手続き　☐ introduce 動 紹介する

56.

What does the woman say will happen tomorrow?
(A) A new employee will start a job.
(B) A business will open at ten o'clock.
(C) A technician will give a presentation.
(D) A manager will order some tools.

女性は、明日何がある予定だと言っていますか。
(A) 新入社員が仕事を始める。
(B) 店が10時に開く。
(C) 技術者がプレゼンをする。
(D) マネージャーが道具を注文する。

▶ 正解　(A)

女性の A new service technician will start work here tomorrow morning.（新しい整備士が、明朝からここで働き始めます）から、(A)が正解。

▶ 言い換えポイント　A new service technician will start work
　→ A new employee will start a job.

57.

Where most likely are the speakers?
(A) At a newspaper
(B) At an auto repair shop
(C) At a travel agency
(D) At a technical school

話し手は、おそらくどこにいますか。
(A) 新聞社
(B) 自動車修理店
(C) 旅行代理店
(D) 技術系専門学校

▶ 正解 (B)

I've got to finish fixing this braking system for a customer（私はこのブレーキ装置の修理をお客様のために終えなければなりません）や to complete the work on that car（その車の作業を終えるのに）などから、話し手は自動車修理店にいることがわかる。よって、(B) が正解。

☐ technical school　技術系専門学校

58.

What must Raymond do by ten o'clock?
(A) Introduce a system
(B) Make a repair
(C) Sign a contract
(D) Arrange some tools

Raymond は、10時までに何をしなければなりませんか。
(A) システムを導入する
(B) 修理を行う
(C) 契約書に署名する
(D) 工具を並べる

▶ 正解 (B)

男性 B が Raymond で、彼は、I've got to finish fixing this braking system for a customer by ten tomorrow.（私は明日の10時までに、このブレーキ装置の修理をお客様のために終えなければなりません）と言っているので、(B) が正解。

☐ contract　名 契約書
☐ arrange　動 並べる

▶ 言い換えポイント　fixing this braking system ➡ Make a repair

🎧 1-44

Questions 59 through 61 refer to the following conversation.

M: I almost fell coming up the steps, Andrea! That's not the first time, either. They were slippery one day last week, too. They're unsafe!

W: I know just what you mean. I've also had trouble getting up the steps recently. We've never had so much snow before!

M: My main concern is that someone gets hurt when our shop is closed—when there's no one here to shovel snow.

W: We ought to get a caution sign that tells people to watch their step.

M: You're right. Do you know of any place that carries them?

W: I'll go online and search for one after we clear the steps.

問題59〜61は次の会話に関するものです。

男性：階段を上っていて滑り落ちそうになりました、Andrea。それに、これが初めてではありません。先週も滑りやすい日が1日ありました。安全ではありません。

女性：全く同感です。私も最近階段を上るのに苦労しています。こんなに雪が降ったことはこれまでありませんでした。

男性：私が一番心配しているのは、店が閉まっている時に誰かが怪我をすることです。雪かきをする人が誰もいない時に。

女性：足元に気をつけるように忠告する警告標識を入手するべきです。

男性：その通りですね。取り扱っているところをどこか知っていますか。

女性：階段をきれいにしたら、ネットで探してみます。

- □ fall　動 転ぶ
- □ slippery　形 滑りやすい
- □ unsafe　形 安全でない
- □ have trouble -ing　〜するのに苦労する
- □ concern　名 心配
- □ get hurt　怪我をする
- □ shovel　動 シャベルですくう
- □ ought to 〜　〜するべきである
- □ caution　名 警告
- □ carry　動 (商品として) 取り扱う

59.

Why does the woman say, "I know just what you mean"?
(A) She feels the same way as the man.
(B) She would like some more details.
(C) She understands the steps in a process.
(D) She has already heard what happened.

女性はなぜ、"I know just what you mean" と言っていますか。
(A) 男性と同じように感じている。
(B) もう少し詳細を知りたい。
(C) 過程における手順を理解している。
(D) 何が起こったかをすでに聞いている。

▶ 正解　(A)

階段が滑りやすく危険であるという発言を受けて、女性はI know just what you mean. と述べ、I've also had trouble getting up the steps recently. (私も最近階段を上るのに苦労しています) と言っている。ここから女性も男性と同じ意見であることがわかるので、(A)が正解。

- □ detail　名 詳細
- □ process　名 過程

60.

Why is the man concerned?
(A) A customer might complain.
(B) The weather may get worse.
(C) Someone could be injured.
(D) Some snow is too deep.

男性はなぜ心配していますか。
(A) 顧客が不満を言うかもしれない。
(B) 天気が悪化するかもしれない。
(C) 誰かが怪我をするかもしれない。
(D) 雪があまりにも深い。

▶ 正解 (C)

男性は、My main concern is that someone gets hurt when our shop is closed（私が一番心配しているのは、店が閉まっている時に誰かが怪我をすることです）と言っているので、(C) が正解。

- complain 動 不満を言う
- injure 動 怪我をさせる

▶ 言い換えポイント　gets hurt ➡ be injured

61.

What does the woman suggest they do?
(A) Close an entrance
(B) Wash some steps
(C) Bring some shovels
(D) Get a sign

女性は、彼らが何をすることを提案していますか。
(A) 入口を閉める
(B) 階段を洗う
(C) シャベルを持ってくる
(D) 標識を入手する

▶ 正解 (D)

女性は、We ought to get a caution sign that tells people to watch their step.（足元に気をつけるように忠告する警告標識を入手すべきです）と言っているので、(D) が正解。

Questions 62 through 64 refer to the following conversation and floor plan.

W: Which room do you think we should paint first? I'd like to start in 304. And after we finish painting that big room, we can work in the others.

M: The manager said we can't go in that room today. There're still guests staying in there. They'll check out tomorrow morning.

W: Then let's start with the room at the end of the hallway. Later today, we'll paint the two smaller rooms. Tomorrow, we'll paint 304.

M: That sounds good to me. I'll go get our supplies, and then I want to put plastic over the beds and tables.

問題62~64は次の会話と間取図に関するものです。

女性：どの部屋を最初に塗装したほうがいいと思いますか。私は304号室から始めたいと思います。そして、その大きい部屋を塗装し終わった後で、他の部屋に取りかかれます。

男性：支配人が言うには、今日はその部屋には入れないそうです。まだ宿泊しているお客様がいます。彼らは明朝チェックアウトします。

女性：それなら廊下の突き当たりの部屋から始めましょう。今日、後で小さい2部屋を塗って、明日、304号室をやりましょう。

男性：いいですね。用品を取りに行ってきて、それからベッドとテーブルにビニールをかけたいと思います。

□ paint 動 ペンキを塗る　□ hallway 名 廊下　□ supply 名 用品　□ plastic 名 ビニール

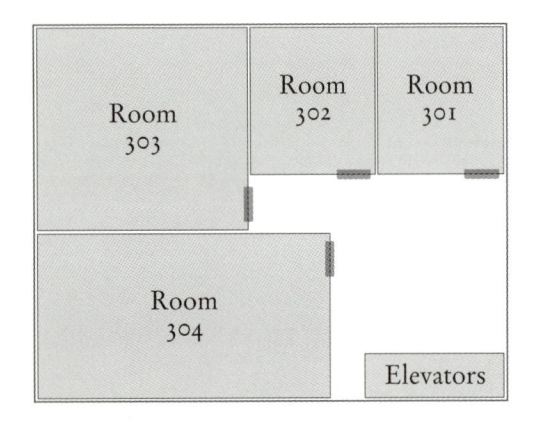

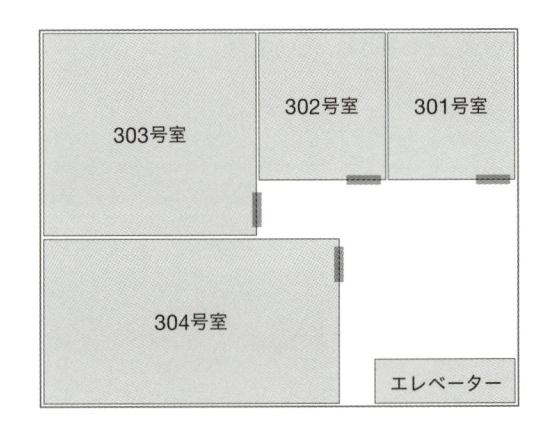

Room 303	Room 302	Room 301
Room 304		Elevators

303号室	302号室	301号室
304号室		エレベーター

62.

What does the man say about the big room?
(A) It is occupied.
(B) It is decorated.
(C) It is comfortable.
(D) It is unlocked.

男性は、大きい部屋について何と言っていますか。
(A) 使用中である。
(B) 飾り付けがされている。
(C) 快適である。
(D) 鍵がかかっていない。

▶ 正解 (A)

大きい部屋の話をする中で、男性はThere're still guests staying in there.（まだ宿泊しているお客様がいます）と言っているので、(A)が正解。

▶ 言い換えポイント　staying in there ➡ It is occupied

- occupy　動（場所を）使用する
- decorate　動 飾る
- comfortable　形 快適な
- unlocked　形 鍵のかかっていない

63.

Look at the graphic. Which room will the speakers paint first?
(A) Room 301
(B) Room 302
(C) Room 303
(D) Room 304

図を見てください。話し手はどの部屋を最初に塗装しますか。
(A) 301号室
(B) 302号室
(C) 303号室
(D) 304号室

▶ 正解 (C)

女性のThen let's start with the room at the end of the hallway.（それなら廊下の突き当たりの部屋から始めましょう）から、最初に塗装するのは、廊下の突き当たりの303号室であることがわかる。

64.

What does the man want to do?
(A) Cover some furniture
(B) Wait for a manager
(C) Check a guest book
(D) Remove some plastic

男性は何をしたいですか。
(A) 家具にカバーをかける
(B) 支配人を待つ
(C) 宿帳を調べる
(D) ビニールを取り除く

▶ 正解 (A)

男性は、I want to put plastic over the beds and tables.（ベッドとテーブルにビニールをかけたいと思います）と言っているので、(A)が正解。このplasticはplastic sheet（ビニールシート）のこと。

▶ 言い換えポイント　put plastic over the beds and tables ➡ Cover some furniture

- cover　動 カバーをかける
- furniture　名 家具
- guest book　宿帳
- remove　動 取り除く

Questions 65 through 67 refer to the following conversation and program.

M: If everyone could take their seats… Since we have lots of issues to cover, I want to get started right away. You should have all received the agenda for this meeting, and, um… Let me see here… Yes, John has some updates about next Tuesday's product launch.

W: Ah… sorry to interrupt, but there's no mention on the agenda about tomorrow's training seminars.

M: Oh, you're right. Let's get that out of the way first. There's going to be a change in the seminar order. Pamela's will be last, since she has to discuss some matters with our Web developer after the lunch break. And David, who's giving the seminar on our sales approaches, will take her time slot. I think that's it, right, Cathy?

W: Yeah, that's all. Go ahead John…

問題65〜67は次の会話とプログラムに関するものです。

男性：みなさん、席に着いてください。取り上げる議題が多いので、さっそく始めたいと思います。みなさんは会議の議題表を受け取っているはずです。そして、ええと、これによると、そう、Johnから来週火曜日の商品発売についての最新情報があります。

女性：あの、話の途中にすみませんが、議題表で明日の研修セミナーについてまったく触れられていません。

男性：ああ、そうですね。まずはそれから片付けましょう。セミナーの順番に変更があります。Pamelaは昼休みの後にウェブ開発者と打ち合わせがあるので、最後になります。そして、我々の販売アプローチについて話すDavidが彼女の時間枠に入ります。以上ですよね、Cathy。

女性：ええ、以上です。進めて下さい、John。

- □ cover 動（話題を）取り上げる □ agenda 名 議題表 □ update 名 最新情報
- □ launch 名 発売 □ interrupt 動 妨げる □ mention 動 言及 □ developer 名 開発者
- □ approach 名 取り組み方 □ time slot 時間枠

SEMINARS	
LEADER	TIME
John Higgins	9:30–10:50
Derrick Hunter	11:00–12:30
Lunch	12:30–1:00
Pamela Plummer	1:00–2:45
David Robinson	3:00–4:45

セミナー	
進行役	時間
John Higgins	9:30–10:50
Derrick Hunter	11:00–12:30
昼休み	12:30–1:00
Pamela Plummer	1:00–2:45
David Robinson	3:00–4:45

65.

Why does the man want to start immediately?
(A) They have a number of topics to discuss.
(B) A registration deadline is approaching.
(C) He has to attend another meeting.
(D) They are expected in a seminar room before 9:30.

なぜ男性はすぐに始めたがっていますか。
(A) 話し合う議題がたくさんある。
(B) 登録期限が近づいている。
(C) 彼は別の会議に出席しなければならない。
(D) 彼らは9時30分より前にセミナー室に行くことになっている。

▶ **正解 (A)**

男性のSince we have lots of issues to cover, I want to get started right away.（取り上げる議題が多いので、さっそく始めたいと思います）から、(A)が正解。

- immediately 副 すぐに
- a number of ～ 多くの～
- registration 名 登録
- deadline 名 期限
- approach 動 近づく

▶ 言い換えポイント　lots of issues to cover
　　　　　　　　　➡ a number of topics to discuss

66.

What does the woman bring to the man's attention?
(A) A topic is not on an agenda.
(B) A product launch needs to be discussed first.
(C) There is an error on a Web site.
(D) Some seminars may take longer than planned.

女性は、男性に何を注目させていますか。
(A) ある事項が議題表に載っていない。
(B) 最初に商品発売について話し合う必要がある。
(C) ウェブサイトに誤りがある。
(D) いくつかのセミナーが予定より長くかかるかもしれない。

▶ **正解 (A)**

女性のsorry to interrupt, but there's no mention on the agenda about tomorrow's training seminars.（話の途中にすみませんが、議題表で明日の研修セミナーについてまったく触れられていません）から、(A)が正解。

- attention 名 注意

▶ 言い換えポイント　no mention on the agenda ➡ not on an agenda

67.

Look at the graphic. Who will lead a seminar starting at one o'clock?
(A) Mr. Higgins
(B) Mr. Hunter
(C) Ms. Plummer
(D) Mr. Robinson

図を見てください。1時から始まるセミナーの進行役を務めるのは誰ですか。
(A) Higginsさん
(B) Hunterさん
(C) Plummerさん
(D) Robinsonさん

▶ **正解 (D)**

スケジュール上では、1時に始まるセミナーの進行役はPamela Plummerとなっているが、代わりにDavidが彼女の時間枠に入ることを男性が述べている。Davidの姓は、Robinsonであることがスケジュール表からわかるので、(D)が正解。

- lead 動 進行役を務める

🎧 1-47

Questions 68 through 70 refer to the following conversation and coupon.

問題68〜70は次の会話とクーポンに関するものです。

W: Hi! I can't believe so many people are coming to the gym today!

M: Hello. Yes—Saturday's always been busy for us.

W: I used to be a member here, but I never came on the weekend.

M: Oh, did you have a weekday-only membership?

W: That's right, and I'm considering getting a new one—maybe next month.

M: I see. Well, how can I help you today?

W: I'm here for the ten o'clock aerobics class. Non-members can join it for $18.00, right? Plus, I have this coupon.

M: Oh, you can't use that right now—sorry. Besides, the next class is full.

W: I see.

M: There'll be another one—at two—you can sign up for, but we'd have to charge you the full price.

女性：こんにちは。こんなに大勢の人が今日ジムに来ているなんて信じられません。

男性：こんにちは。ええ、土曜日はいつも混み合っています。

女性：以前ここの会員でしたが、週末には一度も来ませんでした。

男性：ああ、平日限定会員のご契約でしたか。

女性：そうです、そしてまた新たに会員になろうと考えています。多分来月に。

男性：そうですか。それで、本日はどのようなご用件でしょうか。

女性：10時のエアロビクスのクラスに来ました。会員でなくても18ドル払えば参加できますよね。それと、このクーポンがあります。

男性：ああ、それは現在ご利用いただけません。申し訳ありません。それに、次のクラスは定員に達しています。

女性：そうですか。

男性：また別のクラスがあります。2時になりますが。それにお申し込みいただけますが、正規料金がかかってしまいます。

- ☐ consider 動 検討する
- ☐ besides 副 それに
- ☐ sign up for 〜 〜に申し込む
- ☐ charge 動 請求する

WREN'S GYM
3887 SW King Ave., Portland, OR

$6.00 OFF an Aerobics Class

Anyone can join!
Valid Monday thru Friday.
Coupon can be used only once.

WREN'S GYM
3887 SW King Ave., Portland, OR

エアロビクスのクラスが **6ドル割引**

どなたでも参加できます。
月曜日から金曜日まで有効。
クーポンは1回のみ使用可。

68.

Why is the woman surprised?
(A) Her membership has expired.
(B) The health club is busy.
(C) A class was cancelled.
(D) The man still remembers her.

女性はなぜ驚いていますか。
(A) 彼女の会員権が期限切れである。
(B) ヘルスクラブが混み合っている。
(C) クラスが中止になった。
(D) 男性がまだ彼女のことを覚えている。

▶ **正解** (B)

女性のI can't believe so many people are coming to the gym today!（こんなに大勢の人が今日ジムに来ているなんて信じられません）から、(B)が正解。

- expire 動 （期限が）切れる
- cancel 動 中止する

▶ 言い換えポイント so many people ➡ busy

69.

Look at the graphic. Why is the woman unable to use the coupon?
(A) It is for a different type of class.
(B) She has already used the coupon once.
(C) She must first renew her membership.
(D) It is not valid on Saturday.

図を見てください。女性はなぜクーポンを使えないのですか。
(A) それは異なる種類のクラス用である。
(B) 彼女はクーポンをすでに1度使っている。
(C) 彼女はまず会員権を更新しなければならない。
(D) それは土曜日には有効でない。

▶ **正解** (D)

会話からこの日が土曜日であることがわかるが、クーポンにはValid Monday thru Friday.（月曜日から金曜日まで有効）と記載されているので、土曜日には使えない。よって、(D)が正解。

- unable 形 できない
- renew 動 更新する

▶ 言い換えポイント Valid Monday thru Friday
　　　　　　　　　➡ not valid on Saturday

70.

What does the man say the woman can do?
(A) See a price list
(B) Sign up for another class
(C) Avoid some charges
(D) Take a class schedule

男性は、女性は何ができると言っていますか。
(A) 価格表を見る
(B) 別のクラスに申し込む
(C) 課金を避ける
(D) クラスの予定表をもらう

▶ **正解** (B)

男性は、There'll be another one — at two — you can sign up for（また別のクラスがあります。2時になりますが。それにお申し込みいただけます）と言っているので、(B)が正解。

- avoid 動 避ける

Part 4

解答・解説

🎧 1-49 🇬🇧

Questions 71 through 73 refer to the following telephone message.

Hi, Tim. I'm at the station. You were right—we should've bought tickets sooner. There aren't any seats open on the one we wanted, leaving at 7:30. So, we'll have to go earlier. I'll get two tickets for the 6:15 train. Since we'll arrive in Birmingham two hours before the meeting, let's go to a café first. We'll have some coffee and prepare for our sales presentation. Then, we'll walk to the client's office. Please call me back so we can decide on a place here to meet in the morning. Thanks!

問題71〜73は次の電話のメッセージに関するものです。

もしもし、Tim。私は駅にいます。あなたの言う通りでした。もっと早く切符を買うべきでした。私たちが乗りたかった7時30分発には全く空席がありません。なので、もっと早く行かなければなりません。6時15分の列車の切符を2枚買います。会議の2時間前にBirminghamに到着するので、まずはカフェに行きましょう。コーヒーを飲んで、販売プレゼンに備えましょう。それから、顧客のオフィスへ歩いて行きます。朝ここでの待ち合わせ場所を決めたいので、折り返し電話をください。では。

- □ open 形 空いている
- □ leave 動 出発する
- □ arrive 動 到着する
- □ call 〜 back 〜に折り返し電話をする
- □ decide 動 決める

71. 🇺🇸

Where is the speaker calling from?
(A) An office building
(B) An airport
(C) A café
(D) A train station

話し手は、どこから電話をかけていますか。
(A) オフィスビル
(B) 空港
(C) カフェ
(D) 鉄道の駅

▶ **正解 (D)**

I'm at the station.（私は駅にいます）やI'll get two tickets for the 6:15 train.（6時15分の列車の切符を2枚買います）から、話し手はtrain station（鉄道の駅）にいることがわかるので、(D)が正解。

72.

What time will the woman probably leave for Birmingham?
(A) At 6:15
(B) At 7:30
(C) At 1:00
(D) At 2:00

女性はおそらく何時にBirminghamに向けて出発しますか。
(A) 6時15分に
(B) 7時30分に
(C) 1時に
(D) 2時に

▶ 正解　(A)

I'll get two tickets for the 6:15 train.（6時15分の列車の切符を2枚買います）から、6時15分発の列車に乗ると予想できるので、(A)が正解。

73.

What does the speaker plan to do in Birmingham?
(A) Dine with a client
(B) Stay at a hotel
(C) Give a presentation
(D) Inspect a building

話し手は、Birminghamで何をする予定ですか。
(A) 顧客と食事をする
(B) ホテルに滞在する
(C) プレゼンをする
(D) 建物を検査する

▶ 正解　(C)

We'll have some coffee and prepare for our sales presentation.（コーヒーを飲んで、販売プレゼンに備えましょう）とあるので、プレゼンを行うことがわかる。よって、(C)が正解。

☐ **dine**　動 食事をする
☐ **inspect**　動 検査する

Questions 74 through 76 refer to the following talk.

Good morning. Ben Arnolds is running late. He's now on his way to the factory to show you how to operate our new packaging equipment, and he'll be here soon. While you're waiting, please pick up a manual. They're on the table. When Ben called, he said you should have a look at the diagram on page six. Also, read over the list of machine components on page seven. Later, you will learn what each part is for. Oh, since there isn't a copy for everyone, would you share one with the person beside you? OK, go ahead and get started.

問題74〜76は次の話に関するものです。

おはようございます。Ben Arnoldsは遅れています。彼は、新しい包装機器の操作方法を皆さんに見せるために、現在工場へ向かっている途中で、もうすぐここに到着します。待っている間に、マニュアルを1部取ってください。テーブルの上にあります。Benは、電話してきた際に、皆さんが6ページの図を見ておくべきだと言っていました。また、7ページの機械部品リストに目を通してください。後ほど、各部品の役割を学びます。ああ、全員分の冊子がないので、隣の人と一緒に使ってもらえますか。さあ、それでは始めてください。

- □ **be running late** 遅れている
- □ **on one's way to 〜** 〜への道中である
- □ **package** 動 包装する
- □ **have a look at 〜** 〜を見る
- □ **diagram** 名 図
- □ **component** 名 部品
- □ **share** 動 共有する

74.

What is the main purpose of the talk?
(A) To report some mistakes
(B) To announce a job opportunity
(C) To introduce a guest speaker
(D) To provide some instructions

話の主な目的は何ですか。
(A) 間違いを報告すること
(B) 雇用機会を知らせること
(C) ゲストスピーカーを紹介すること
(D) 指示を伝えること

▶ **正解　(D)**

you should have a look at the diagram on page six.（皆さんが6ページの図を見ておくべきだ）やread over the list of machine components on page seven.（7ページの機械部品リストに目を通してください）など、話し手は講習を受ける前にすべきことを伝えているので、(D)が正解。

- □ **report** 動 報告する
- □ **opportunity** 名 機会
- □ **instructions** 名 （複数形で）指示

Part 4 | 解答・解説

75.

According to the speaker, what will happen soon?
(A) Some machine parts will be installed.
(B) Mr. Arnolds will give a demonstration.
(C) The listeners will look at a drawing of a facility.
(D) An illustration will be displayed on a screen.

話し手によると、もうすぐ何が起こりますか。
(A) いくつかの機械部品が取り付けられる。
(B) Arnoldsさんが実演をする。
(C) 聞き手が施設の図面を見る。
(D) イラストがスクリーンに映し出される。

▶ 正解 (B)

He's now on his way to the factory to show you how to operate our new packaging equipment, and he'll be here soon. (彼は、新しい包装機器の操作方法を皆さんに見せるために、現在工場へ向かっている途中で、もうすぐここに到着します)と言っている。「新しい包装機器の操作方法を見せる」というのは、実際に装置を操作して実演するということなので、(B)が正解。

- □ **install** 動 取り付ける
- □ **give a demonstration** 実演を行う
- □ **facility** 名 施設
- □ **illustration** 名 イラスト
- □ **display** 動 映し出す

76.

What does the speaker ask the listeners to do?
(A) Operate a machine
(B) Complete a list
(C) Unwrap a package
(D) Share a manual

話し手は、聞き手に何をするよう頼んでいますか。
(A) 機械を操作する
(B) リストを完成させる
(C) 小包の包装を解く
(D) マニュアルを人と一緒に使う

▶ 正解 (D)

since there isn't a copy for everyone, would you share one with the person beside you? (全員分の冊子がないので、隣の人と一緒に使ってもらえますか)と言っており、このoneはa manual(マニュアル)を指すので、(D)が正解。

- □ **complete** 動 完成させる
- □ **unwrap** 動 包装を取る

89

🎧 1-51

Questions 77 through 79 refer to the following news report.

In other news, *Urban Lifestyles* has rated Irving as the fourth best place to live in the country. The magazine publishes its list every year. Abura City was rated as the best. The cities of Huntston and Portgomery follow in second and third place, respectively. Our city, Irving, comes next. An editor at the magazine wrote that several factors influenced their decision, including our excellent parks and public transport system. And even though Irving didn't make the top spot, we should be proud that our home has been acknowledged. OK, now let's get a traffic update…

問題77～79は次のニュース報道に関するものです。

その他のニュースですが、*Urban Lifestyles* はIrvingを国内で4番目に住むのによい場所として評価しました。同誌は毎年リストを発表しています。Abura市が最高の評価を受けました。続いてHuntston市とPortgomery市が、それぞれ2位と3位です。私たちの市、Irvingはその次に来ています。雑誌の編集者は、市の素晴らしい公園と公共輸送機関を含むいくつかの要因が判定に影響したと書いています。そして、Irvingは首位にはならなかったものの、私たちは地元が認められたことを誇りに思うべきです。では、次に最新の道路交通情報です。

- □ **rate** 動 評価する
- □ **respectively** 副 それぞれ
- □ **factor** 名 要因
- □ **influence** 動 影響する
- □ **decision** 名 判定
- □ **acknowledge** 動 認める

77.

What does the speaker announce?
(A) A magazine launch
(B) A publishing date
(C) A new tourist destination
(D) A ranking of cities

話し手は、何を発表していますか。
(A) 雑誌の創刊
(B) 出版日
(C) 新しい観光地
(D) 都市のランキング

▶ 正解 **(D)**

このニュースでは、ある雑誌が発表した「住むのによい都市ランキング」の結果を伝えており、上位に入った都市名が挙げられている。よって、(D)が正解。

- □ **launch** 名 （雑誌の）創刊
- □ **destination** 名 目的地

78.

Where is the broadcast being made?
(A) Abura
(B) Huntston
(C) Portgomery
(D) Irving

放送はどこで行われていますか。
(A) Abura
(B) Huntston
(C) Portgomery
(D) Irving

▶ 正解　(D)

Our city, Irving, comes next.（私たちの市、Irvingはその次に来ています）と言っているので、この放送はIrvingで行われていることがわかる。よって、(D)が正解。

☐ **broadcast**　名 放送

79.

According to the speaker, why should the listeners be proud?
(A) A local writer won a prize.
(B) Many tourists have been visiting their city.
(C) Their city was recognized as a good place to live.
(D) Their mayor was honored with an award.

話し手によると、聞き手はなぜ誇りに思うべきですか。
(A) 地元の作家が賞を取った。
(B) 多くの観光客が市を訪問している。
(C) 彼らの市が住むのによい場所だと認められた。
(D) 市長が賞を授けられた。

▶ 正解　(C)

Irvingが国内で4番目に住むのによい場所として評価されたことを受け、we should be proud that our home has been acknowledged.（私たちは地元が認められたことを誇りに思うべきです）と言っているので、(C)が正解。

☐ **recognize**　動 認める

▶ 言い換えポイント　acknowledged ➡ recognized

🎧 1-52

Questions 80 through 82 refer to the following introduction.

Welcome aboard! My name is Georgina. This is David, your driver. Our first stop will be the Abrams Courthouse—a very old Abramsville building. Inside, I'll show you around, and afterward, David will take us to another historical area, where some of the first settlers in the town set up stores many years ago. We will have lunch at McDougal's Corral, the famous diner. After that, we'll head over to the port. We'll stay there for an hour before returning to the hotel. Please feel free to leave any belongings here during the tour, as David will lock the door at each stop. And thank you so much for joining us today!

問題80〜82は次の紹介に関するものです。

ご乗車ありがとうございます。私の名前はGeorginaです。こちらは運転手のDavidです。最初に停車するのはAbrams CourthouseでAbramsvilleの非常に古い建物です。私が皆さんにその中をご案内し、その後Davidが、町の最初の入植者がずっと前に店を建てた歴史的地区に皆さんをお連れします。有名な食堂であるMcDougal's Corralで昼食をとります。その後、港に向かいます。ホテルに戻る前に、そこで1時間過ごします。Davidが各停車スポットでドアをロックしますので、ツアー中はどんな所持品もどうぞご自由にここに置いていってください。そして本日はご参加いただきありがとうございます。

- □ aboard 副 乗車して □ courthouse 名 裁判所 □ historical 形 歴史的な
- □ settler 名 入植者 □ set up 建てる □ corral 名 囲い □ leave 動 残す
- □ belongings 名 所持品 □ lock 動 鍵をかける

80.

Who most likely is the speaker?
(A) A tour guide
(B) A hotel clerk
(C) A restaurant owner
(D) A bus driver

話し手はおそらく誰ですか。
(A) ツアーガイド
(B) ホテルのフロント係
(C) レストランのオーナー
(D) バスの運転手

▶ 正解 (A)

話し手はまず自分の名前を告げ、ドライバーを紹介し、ツアーの行程を説明していることから、(A) A tour guide (ツアーガイド) であるとわかる。

81.

Where will the listeners go after lunch?
(A) To a courthouse
(B) To a port
(C) To a store
(D) To a museum

聞き手は昼食の後はどこに行きますか。
(A) 裁判所に
(B) 港に
(C) 店に
(D) 博物館に

▶ 正解 (B)

有名な食堂で昼食をとると伝えた後、After that, we'll head over to the port. (その後、港に向かいます) と言っているので、(B)が正解。

82.

According to the speaker, what can the listeners do?
(A) View a historical document
(B) Leave behind personal belongings
(C) Take pictures inside some shops
(D) Participate in an activity for free

話し手によると、聞き手は何をすることができますか。
(A) 歴史的な文書を見る
(B) 私物を置いていく
(C) 何軒かの店内で写真を撮る
(D) 無料で活動に参加する

▶ 正解 (B)

Please feel free to leave any belongings here during the tour (ツアー中はどんな所持品もどうぞご自由にここに置いていってください) と言っているので、(B)を選ぶ。

🎧 1-53

Questions 83 through 85 refer to the following speech.

Welcome to Briarwood Park's annual volunteer appreciation barbecue! Over the past year, you have kept this park clean and beautiful. Together, you've spent hundreds of hours planting, weeding, mowing, and doing much more. You're always willing to lend a hand. So, today, the Parks Commission thanks you for all your hard work! Vivian and Brian will now hand out plastic cutlery and paper plates. After that, come over to these picnic tables and help yourself to whatever you'd like. Cups and drinks are on the table to my left. Please enjoy the afternoon!

問題83〜85は次のスピーチに関するものです。

Briarwood Parkの年次ボランティア感謝バーベキューにようこそ。この1年間、皆さんはこの公園を清潔に、そして美しく保ってくださいました。一緒に植物を植えたり、雑草を除去したり、芝刈りをしたり、さらに多くのことをするのに何百時間も費やしました。皆さんは常に進んで手を貸してくださいます。ですから、本日、Parks Commissionは、皆さんの全てのご苦労に感謝いたします。ではVivianとBrianがプラスチックのナイフやフォークと紙皿を配ります。その後、こちらのピクニックテーブルに来て、お好きなものをご自由にどうぞ。カップと飲み物は、私の左側のテーブルにあります。楽しい午後をお過ごしください。

- □ **annual** 形 年次の
- □ **appreciation** 名 感謝
- □ **plant** 動 植える
- □ **weed** 動 雑草を除去する
- □ **mow** 動 刈り取る
- □ **lend a hand** 手を貸す、手伝う
- □ **commission** 名 委員会
- □ **cutlery** 名 ナイフやフォークなどの食卓食器類

83.

What is the main purpose of the event?
(A) To celebrate the anniversary of a park
(B) To attract visitors to the area
(C) To show gratitude to some volunteers
(D) To prepare for some outdoor projects

イベントの主な目的は何ですか。
(A) 公園の記念日を祝うこと
(B) 地域に訪問客を引き付けること
(C) ボランティアに感謝の意を表すこと
(D) 屋外のプロジェクトに備えること

▶ 正解 **(C)**

ボランティアの功績や姿勢をたたえ、So, today, the Parks Commission thanks you for all your hard work!（ですから、本日、Parks Commissionは、皆さんの全てのご苦労に感謝いたします）と言っているので、(C)が正解。

- □ **attract** 動 引き付ける
- □ **gratitude** 名 感謝

▶ 言い換えポイント　thanks ➡ show gratitude

84.

What does the speaker mean when she says, "and doing much more"?

(A) The listeners did more work than they were assigned.
(B) The listeners did a lot more volunteer work this year.
(C) The listeners are expected to participate again next year.
(D) The listeners carried out numerous other tasks as well.

話し手が "and doing much more" と言っているのはどういう意味ですか。

(A) 聞き手が割り当てられたよりも多くの作業をした。
(B) 聞き手が今年、より多くのボランティア活動をした。
(C) 聞き手が来年再び参加すると期待されている。
(D) 聞き手が多数の他の仕事も行った。

▶ 正解 (D)

you've spent hundreds of hours planting, weeding, mowing, and doing much more. という流れで使われているので、and doing much more は「一緒に植物を植えたり、雑草を除去したり、芝刈りをしたり」に加え、さらに多くのことを行ったという意味になり、(D)が正解。

□ **assign** 動 割り当てる
□ **participate** 動 参加する
□ **carry out** 遂行する

85.

What will the listeners most likely do next?
(A) Have a meal
(B) Move a table
(C) Help visitors
(D) Clean dishes

聞き手は次におそらく何をしますか。
(A) 食事をとる
(B) テーブルを動かす
(C) 訪問者に手助けをする
(D) 食器を洗う

▶ 正解 (A)

プラスチックのナイフやフォークと紙皿を配ると述べた後、After that, come over to these picnic tables and help yourself to whatever you'd like. (その後、こちらのピクニックテーブルに来て、お好きなものをご自由にどうぞ) と言っているので、聞き手がこれから食事をすることがわかる。

🎧 1-54

Questions 86 through 88 refer to the following telephone message.

Hello, this is a message for Alonzo Meredith. It's Tanya Winston calling from the *Palmdale Times*. We're sorry that your business's advertisement did not appear in our publication on one of the days you had requested. That was my mistake, as I misread a date on the form you filled out for us. We will of course refund some of the fee you paid for printing the advertisement. In addition, we'd like to place your advertisement—at no cost to you—on the sixth page of our February 18 edition. If you'd like to accept this offer, please let me know by Thursday. Thank you.

問題86〜88は次の電話のメッセージに関するものです。

もしもし、これはAlonzo Meredithさんへの伝言です。こちらは*Palmdale Times*のTanya Winstonです。御社の広告が、ご依頼いただいた期間中の1日、当紙に掲載されなかったことをお詫び申し上げます。私が御社にご記入いただいた用紙の日付を読み誤ったため起こったもので、私の誤りでございました。もちろん、御社が広告を印刷するために払った料金の一部を払い戻しいたします。さらに、2月18日版の6ページに無料で御社の広告を掲載させていただきたいと思います。この申し出をお受けになる場合は、木曜日までにお知らせいただけますでしょうか。失礼いたします。

- □ publication 名 出版物　□ request 動 依頼する　□ misread 動 読み違える
- □ fill out 記入する　□ refund 動 返金する　□ place 動 載せる　□ at no cost 無料で
- □ accept 動 承諾する

86.

Why does the caller apologize?
(A) A newspaper was delivered to the wrong address.
(B) An advertisement was not placed as requested.
(C) A date in an article was incorrect.
(D) A document was not properly formatted.

電話をかけている人はなぜ謝罪していますか。
(A) 新聞が間違った住所に届けられた。
(B) 広告が依頼された通りに掲載されなかった。
(C) 記事中の日付が間違っていた。
(D) 文書が適切に書式設定されなかった。

▶ 正解 (B)

We're sorry that your business's advertisement did not appear in our publication on one of the days you had requested.（御社の広告が、ご依頼いただいた期間中の1日、当紙に掲載されなかったことをお詫び申し上げます）とあるので、(B)が正解。

- □ apologize 動 謝罪する
- □ deliver 動 配達する
- □ properly 副 適切に
- □ format 動 書式設定する

▶ 言い換えポイント　your business's advertisement did not appear
　➡ An advertisement was not placed

87.

What does the caller say happened?
(A) She did not read some information correctly.
(B) She was told to choose a date in February.
(C) She met with Mr. Meredith on a Saturday.
(D) She was unable to fill out a form completely.

電話をかけている人は、何があったと言っていますか。
(A) 情報を正しく読まなかった。
(B) 2月のある1日を選ぶように言われた。
(C) ある土曜日にMeredithさんと会った。
(D) 用紙に完全に記入できなかった。

▶ 正解 (A)

間違えが起こった理由をI misread a date on the form you filled out for us.（私が御社にご記入いただいた用紙の日付を読み誤った）と説明しているので、(A)が正解。

□ correctly　副 正しく
□ completely　副 完全に

▶ 言い換えポイント　misread a date
　➡ did not read some information correctly

88.

What is the caller offering?
(A) Subscription discounts
(B) Free advertising space
(C) Copies of a newspaper
(D) Design suggestions

電話をかけている人は、何を申し出ていますか。
(A) 定期購読の割引
(B) 無料の広告スペース
(C) 新聞数部
(D) デザインの提案

▶ 正解 (B)

we'd like to place your advertisement — at no cost to you — on the sixth page of our February 18 edition.（2月18日版の6ページに無料で御社の広告を掲載させていただきたいと思います）から、(B)が正解。

□ subscription　名 購読
□ suggestion　名 提案

▶ 言い換えポイント　place your advertisement at no cost
　➡ Free advertising space

1-55

Questions 89 through 91 refer to the following advertisement.

Picture your dream home… Is it a beachfront property with a view of the sea? Or perhaps it's a cozy house in the suburbs with a white picket fence. At Greene Realtors, we can turn your dream into reality. With over six thousand properties, we offer a huge selection compared to other agencies. But Greene's experienced real estate agents are what people appreciate most about us. They will help you find a property, and they will help you secure the financing to buy it, too! Need I say more? Stop by our office at 59 Wallingford Road or call us at 555-7944 today to schedule an appointment.

問題89～91は次の広告に関するものです。

あなたの理想の家を思い描いてください。それは、海を眺められる海岸沿いの物件ですか。または、白い杭柵に囲まれた郊外の居心地のよい家かもしれません。Greene Realtorsでは、あなたの夢を現実にします。6,000を超える物件を揃えている当社は、他の代理店に比べて豊富な選択肢を提供しています。しかし、当社が最も評価を受けているのは、Greeneの経験豊かな不動産仲介者です。彼らはあなたが物件を見つけるお手伝いをして、また、購入のために資金を確保するお手伝いもします。これ以上言う必要がありますか。59 Wallingford Roadにあるオフィスにお越しになるか、面会の予定を組むために555-7944に本日お電話してください。

- □ property 名 不動産物件
- □ cozy 形 居心地のよい
- □ picket fence 杭柵
- □ realtor 名 不動産業者
- □ compared to ～ ～と比べて
- □ agency 名 代理店
- □ experienced 形 経験豊富な
- □ real estate agent 不動産仲介者
- □ appreciate 動 評価する、感謝する
- □ secure 動 確保する
- □ financing 名 資金、資金調達
- □ stop by 立ち寄る

89.

What type of business is being advertised?
(A) A seaside resort
(B) A home improvement store
(C) A construction company
(D) A real estate agency

どんな種類の事業が広告されていますか。
(A) 海辺のリゾート
(B) ホームセンター
(C) 建設会社
(D) 不動産代理店

▶ 正解 (D)

Greene RealtorsのRealtorには、不動産業者という意味がある。また、全体を通して不動産物件を見つける手伝いをする業者であることがわかるので、(D) A real estate agency（不動産代理店）が正解。

90.

According to the advertisement, what do people like the most about the business?
(A) Its employees
(B) Its selection
(C) Its location
(D) Its prices

広告によれば、人々はこの会社の何を一番気に入っていますか。
(A) 従業員
(B) 品揃え
(C) 場所
(D) 価格

▶ 正解 (A)

But Greene's experienced real estate agents are what people appreciate most about us. (しかし、当社が最も評価を受けているのは、Greeneの経験豊かな不動産仲介者です) とある。彼らはこの会社の従業員なので、(A) が正解。

91.

What does the speaker mean when he says, "Need I say more"?
(A) He cannot reveal a secret.
(B) He wants to describe the business more.
(C) He feels that he has mentioned enough.
(D) He would like to repeat some information.

話し手が "Need I say more" と言っているのはどういう意味ですか。
(A) 秘密を明かすことができない。
(B) 事業についてもっと説明したい。
(C) 十分に話したと感じている。
(D) 情報を繰り返したいと思っている。

▶ 正解 (C)

Greene Realtorsの素晴らしいところを述べてきたのに続いて、Need I say more?と言っているので、「これ以上言う必要がありますか (=ありませんよね)」という意味になる。よって、(C) が正解。

- **reveal** 動 明かす
- **describe** 動 説明する
- **mention** 動 言及する

🎧 1-56

Questions 92 through 94 refer to the following announcement.

Your attention, please! We hope you're enjoying the Victoria Career Fair. The lecture by recruitment consultant James Bennet is about to begin. The session was initially scheduled to take place in the exhibition hall, but it has been moved to the third-floor conference room due to a technical problem with the sound system. Mr. Bennet will talk about how job interviews have changed over the years. He'll explain a number of present-day interview techniques. And he'll also provide lots of advice. So, don't miss out! Come and listen to what he has to say! And prepare to do your best in your next interview.

問題92〜94は次のお知らせに関するものです。

ご案内申し上げます。皆様がVictoria Career Fairをお楽しみいただいていることを願っております。求人コンサルタントのJames Bennetによる講演がまもなく始まります。セッションは当初、展示ホールで行われる予定でしたが、音響システムの技術的な問題により、3階の会議室に移動になりました。Bennetさんは、就職面接が年月と共にどのように変化してきたかについて話します。彼は、今日のたくさんの面接のテクニックについても説明いたします。そして、彼は多くのアドバイスも行います。ですから、この機会を逃さないでください。彼の言うことを聞きに来てください。そして、次回の面接で最善を尽くせるように備えてください。

- □ recruitment 名 求人
- □ initially 副 当初
- □ conference room 会議室
- □ due to 〜 〜が原因で
- □ technical 形 技術上の
- □ present-day 形 今日の
- □ provide 動 与える
- □ miss out 機会を逃す

92.

What is the purpose of the announcement?
(A) To promote a talk
(B) To explain a technique
(C) To describe a job
(D) To report a delay

お知らせの目的は何ですか。
(A) 講演を宣伝すること
(B) 技術を説明すること
(C) 職務内容を説明すること
(D) 遅延を知らせること

▶ 正解 (A)

Bennetさんの講演がこれから始まることが伝えられ、講演の場所や内容が述べられているので、(A) To promote a talk（講演を宣伝すること）が正解。

□ promote 動 宣伝する

93.

Why will Mr. Bennet be using a different room?
(A) A screen was set up in the wrong place.
(B) Some sessions were not scheduled correctly.
(C) Some equipment is not working properly.
(D) A hall is not big enough for an audience.

なぜBennetさんは別の部屋を使いますか。
(A) スクリーンが誤った場所に設置された。
(B) いくつかのセッションが正しく予定を組まれていなかった。
(C) 機器が正しく作動していない。
(D) ホールが観衆を収容するのに十分な広さがない。

▶ 正解 (C)

it has been moved to the third-floor conference room due to a technical problem with the sound system.（音響システムの技術的な問題により、3階の会議室に移動になりました）から、技術的な問題で部屋が変更になったとわかるので、(C)が正解。

▶ 言い換えポイント　a technical problem with the sound system
　➡ equipment is not working properly

□ correctly　副 正しく

94.

What does the speaker mean when she says, "don't miss out"?
(A) Listeners should listen carefully.
(B) Listeners should attend a lecture.
(C) Listeners should not forget some advice.
(D) Listeners should not be unhappy.

話し手が "don't miss out" と言っているのはどういう意味ですか。
(A) 聞き手は、注意して聞くべきである。
(B) 聞き手は、講演に出席すべきである。
(C) 聞き手は、アドバイスを忘れてはならない。
(D) 聞き手は、悲しんでいてはいけない。

▶ 正解 (B)

Bennetさんの講演の説明をした後、don't miss outと言っているので、「その講演を逃さないように（＝その講演を必ず聞きに行くように）」という意味になる。よって、(B)が正解。

🎧 1-57

Questions 95 through 97 refer to the following excerpt from a meeting and chart.

Let's move on to the next item, which is… Ah, yes, the Sales Department received a complaint from David Hewitt. He works at a construction site that we are providing cement to. He called because we sent them eighty bags. They had asked for ninety. Now, his company buys a lot of cement from us. As shown in the chart, they are the second largest customer in terms of the amount of cement purchased from us. That was in September. We can't risk losing business from them over careless mistakes. So, if you're responsible for shipping, make sure that everything we're sending customers is double-checked before it leaves the warehouse.

問題95〜97は会議の一部とグラフに関するものです。

次の議題に移りましょう、議題は、ああ、そうでした、営業部がDavid Hewittから苦情を受けました。彼は、我々がセメントを供給している建設現場で働いています。彼は、我々が80袋送ったので電話してきました。彼らが注文したのは90袋です。現在、彼の会社は我々から多くのセメントを購入しています。グラフで示されているように、彼らは、我々から購入したセメントの量に関して2番目に大きな顧客です。それは9月でした。軽率なミスで彼らとの取引を失う危険を冒すわけにはいきません。ですから、発送の責任者は、顧客に送る全ての物が、倉庫から発送される前に二重にチェックされているか確認してください。

- □ excerpt 名 抜粋
- □ Sales Department 営業部
- □ complaint 名 苦情
- □ provide 動 供給する
- □ in terms of 〜 〜の観点から
- □ purchase 動 購入する
- □ risk 動 危険を冒す
- □ careless 形 軽率な
- □ responsible 形 責任のある
- □ shipping 名 発送
- □ double-check 動 二重にチェックする
- □ warehouse 名 倉庫

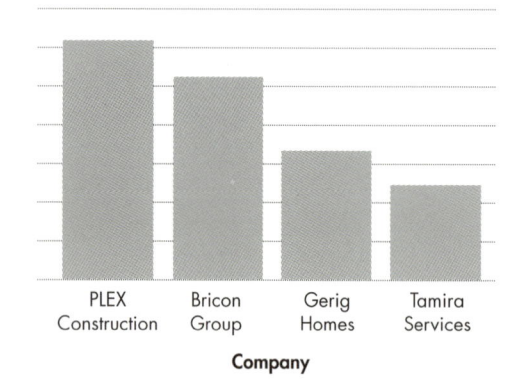

Sales in September

| PLEX Construction | Bricon Group | Gerig Homes | Tamira Services |

Company

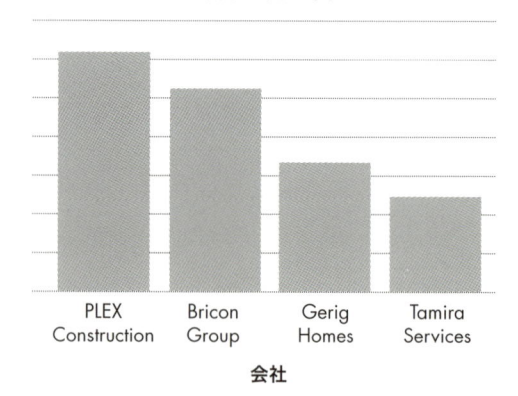

9月の売上高

| PLEX Construction | Bricon Group | Gerig Homes | Tamira Services |

会社

95.

Why did Mr. Hewitt call the Sales Department?
(A) To discuss a billing error
(B) To complain about a shipment
(C) To order additional materials
(D) To inquire about product features

なぜHewittさんは営業部に電話をかけましたか。
(A) 請求の間違いについて話すため
(B) 配送品について苦情を言うため
(C) 追加の資材を注文するため
(D) 製品の機能について尋ねるため

▶ 正解 (B)

Hewittさんが電話をしてきた理由をHe called because we sent them eighty bags. They had asked for ninety.（彼は、我々が80袋送ったので電話してきました。彼らが注文したのは90袋です）と説明しているので、(B)が正解。

- billing 名 請求
- complain 動 苦情を言う
- shipment 名 発送品
- inquire 動 尋ねる
- feature 名 機能、特徴

96.

Look at the graphic. Which company does Mr. Hewitt work for?
(A) PLEX Construction
(B) Bricon Group
(C) Gerig Homes
(D) Tamira Services

図を見てください。Hewittさんはどの会社に勤務していますか。
(A) PLEX Construction
(B) Bricon Group
(C) Gerig Homes
(D) Tamira Services

▶ 正解 (B)

they are the second largest customer in terms of the amount of cement purchased from us. That was in September.（彼らは、我々から購入したセメントの量に関して2番目に大きな顧客です。それは9月でした）から、9月に売上高2位の会社をグラフから探し、(B) Bricon Groupを選ぶ。

97.

What does the speaker tell listeners to do?
(A) Speak directly to construction site supervisors
(B) Keep accurate records of warehouse inventory
(C) Ensure that all shipments are checked twice
(D) Correct errors in some recent sales data

話し手は、聞き手に何をするように言っていますか。
(A) 建設現場の監督と直接話す
(B) 倉庫の在庫の正確な記録をつける
(C) 確実に全ての配送品を2回チェックする
(D) 最近の販売データの間違いを訂正する

▶ 正解 (C)

話し手は発送責任者に対しmake sure that everything we're sending customers is double-checked before it leaves the warehouse.（顧客に送る全ての物が、倉庫から発送される前に二重にチェックされているか確認してください）と言っているので、(C)が正解。

- ensure 動 確実にする
- correct 動 訂正する

▶ 言い換えポイント make sure that everything we're sending customers is double-checked
➡ Ensure that all shipments are checked twice

Questions 98 through 100 refer to the following announcement and schedule.

Attention! Due to a mechanical problem, the Eastbound Ferry did not depart at 8:10 as scheduled. Passengers with a ticket for this ferry may use it for the Westbound Ferry, which is now boarding passengers for its 8:40 departure. Both ferries make the same stops around Ludlow Bay while heading in opposite directions. Ticket holders who wish to receive a refund may do so inside the terminal building. We apologize for the inconvenience. Also, please be aware that the Eastbound Ferry will be ready for its next scheduled departure time.

問題98〜100は次のお知らせとスケジュールに関するものです。

ご案内申し上げます。機械的な故障により、東回りのフェリーは、予定の8時10分に出港できませんでした。このフェリーの乗船券をお持ちのお客様は、8時40分の出港に向けて現在乗船中の西回りのフェリーをご利用いただけます。どちらのフェリーもLudlow湾の同じ場所に停泊しますが、進行方向が逆になります。乗船券をお持ちで払い戻しをご希望の方は、ターミナルの建物内でお手続きができます。ご不便をお詫びいたします。また、東回りのフェリーは次の予定出港時刻までには準備が整いますことにご留意ください。

- □ eastbound 形 東回りの
- □ westbound 形 西回りの
- □ board 動 乗船させる
- □ head 動 進行する
- □ opposite 形 逆の
- □ direction 名 方向
- □ refund 名 払い戻し
- □ apologize 動 詫びる
- □ inconvenience 名 不便
- □ please be aware that 〜 〜にご留意ください

Ludlow Bay Ferries
MORNING DEPARTURE TIMES

Eastbound Ferry	Westbound Ferry
7:10	7:40
8:10	8:40
9:20	10:00
10:40	11:20

Ludlow湾のフェリー
午前中の出港時間

東回りのフェリー	西回りのフェリー
7:10	7:40
8:10	8:40
9:20	10:00
10:40	11:20

Part 4 | 解答・解説

98.

What problem does the speaker announce?
(A) A bus is running late.
(B) A ticket machine is broken.
(C) A tour has been cancelled.
(D) A ferry could not leave.

話し手は、どんな問題を知らせていますか。
(A) バスが遅れている。
(B) 乗船券の販売機が壊れている。
(C) ツアーが中止された。
(D) フェリーが出港できなかった。

▶ 正解　(D)

Due to a mechanical problem, the Eastbound Ferry did not depart at 8:10 as scheduled. (機械的な故障により、東回りのフェリーは、予定の8時10分に出港できませんでした) と言っているので、(D) A ferry could not leave. (フェリーが出港できなかった) が正解。

▶ 言い換えポイント　did not depart ➡ could not leave

99.

According to the speaker, what can some people do?
(A) Get their money back
(B) Transfer to a train
(C) Receive a complimentary ticket
(D) Reach a destination faster

話し手によれば、一部の人々は何ができますか。
(A) 返金を受ける
(B) 電車に乗り換える
(C) 無料の乗船券を受け取る
(D) 目的地により早く到着する

▶ 正解　(A)

Ticket holders who wish to receive a refund may do so inside the terminal building. (乗船券をお持ちで払い戻しをご希望の方は、ターミナルの建物内でお手続きができます) から、(A) が正解。

□ transfer　動 乗り換える
□ complimentary　形 無料の
□ destination　名 目的地

▶ 言い換えポイント　receive a refund ➡ get their money back

100.

Look at the graphic. What time will the next Eastbound Ferry depart?
(A) At 7:10
(B) At 8:10
(C) At 9:20
(D) At 10:40

図を見てください。次の東回りのフェリーは、何時に出港しますか。
(A) 7時10分に
(B) 8時10分に
(C) 9時20分に
(D) 10時40分に

▶ 正解　(C)

最後に the Eastbound Ferry will be ready for its next scheduled departure time. (東回りのフェリーは次の予定出港時刻までには準備が整います) と述べている。前半で8時10分発予定の東回りの便が運航中止となったことが伝えられているので、時刻表から次の出港時刻は9時20分であるとわかる。

105

Part 5 解答・解説

101. 🎧 2-1 🇬🇧

The car manufacturer announced that its convertible will not be available for purchase ------- early next year.

(A) then　それから
(B) about　〜に関して
(C) until　〜まで
(D) since　〜以後

▶ **正解 (C)**

(C) until（〜まで）を使い until early next year（来年初頭まで）とすると、will not be available for purchase（購入可能にならない）と上手くつながる。

- □ **manufacturer** 名 製造業者、メーカー
- □ **purchase** 名 購入

訳　自動車メーカーは、コンバーチブルが来年初頭まで購入可能にならないと発表した。

102. 🎧 2-1 🇬🇧

Business professionals enroll in courses at the Ofra Institute to enhance skills ------- to their jobs.

(A) relevant　関連した
(B) consistent　首尾一貫した
(C) accountable　責任がある
(D) significant　意味のある

▶ **正解 (A)**

(A)を使うと relevant to で「〜に関連した」の意味なので、skills relevant to their jobs で「仕事に関連した」となり意味が通る。relevant to their jobs が前の skills を修飾している。

- □ **enroll in 〜**　〜を受講する
- □ **enhance**　動 高める

訳　ビジネスパーソンは、仕事に関連した技能を高めるために Ofra Institute のコースを受講する。

103. 🎧 2-1 🇬🇧

Visit Wilshire Costume Rentals today ------- our brand-new location in the Magnolia Mall on Westwood Avenue.

(A) to　〜へ
(B) following　〜に続いて
(C) at　〜で／に
(D) before　〜の前に

▶ **正解 (C)**

Visit Wilshire Costume Rentals（Wilshire Costume Rentalsを訪れる）と our brand-new location（開店したばかりの店舗）の間に来る前置詞を選ぶ。(C) at（〜に）を使うと、「開店したばかりの Wilshire Costume Rentals の店舗に」となり上手くつながる。

- □ **brand-new** 形 新しい
- □ **location** 名 店舗

訳　Westwood Avenue の Magnolia Mall に入っている開店したばかりの Wilshire Costume Rentals の店舗に、本日お越しください。

104. 🎧 2-1 🇬🇧

The construction of the building resumed six months after the project was suspended ------- a lack of funding.

(A) as much as　〜と同じ程度に
(B) even so　それでも
(C) as soon as　〜するとすぐに
(D) due to　〜のため

▶ **正解 (D)**

(D) due to は「〜のため」という意味なので、これを使うと、空所前後で「a lack of funding（資金不足）のためプロジェクトが中断された」となり、上手くつながる。

- □ **resume** 動 再開する
- □ **suspend** 動 中断する
- □ **funding** 名 資金

訳　ビルの建設工事は、資金不足のためプロジェクトが中断されてから6ヵ月後に再開した。

105.

Archways Hotel preferred guests can enjoy ------- use of the fitness centers at all locations.

(A) free　無料の、自由にする
(B) freeing　freeの-ing形
(C) freed　freeの過去形・過去分詞
(D) freedom　自由

訳　Archways Hotelの優待客の方は、フィットネスセンターを全店で無料にてご利用いただけます。

▶ 正解　(A)

(A) free（無料の）を使うとfree useで「無料の使用」となり、ホテルのフィットネスセンターの利用に関する文脈に合う。freeは「自由にする」という意味の動詞で使われることもあるが、(B) freeingと(C) freedはuseを修飾する語としては意味的に不適切。

☐ preferred guest　優待客
☐ location　名 店舗

106.

Any employees ------- are interested in the supervisor position may now submit an application.

(A) whose　その人の
(B) who　〜する人
(C) whoever　〜する誰でも
(D) whichever　どちらでも

訳　監督者の職に関心のある従業員は誰でも、応募書類を現在提出することができます。

▶ 正解　(B)

Any employees（従業員は誰でも）を先行詞として受け、後ろのare interested in（関心のある）の主語として機能する語として(B) whoが適切。Any employees who are interested in 〜で「〜に関心のある従業員は誰でも」の意味。

☐ supervisor　名 監督者
☐ submit　動 提出する
☐ application　名 応募書類

107.

The presentations at the symposium featured the world's leading experts on cyber security, ------- Brennen Clayton.

(A) including　include（〜を含む）の-ing形
(B) performing　perform（〜を行う）の-ing形
(C) regarding　regard（〜と見なす）の-ing形、〜に関して
(D) consisting　consist（〜から成る）の-ing形

訳　シンポジウムのプレゼンは、Brennen Claytonを含むサイバーセキュリティの世界一流の専門家たちを呼び物とした。

▶ 正解　(A)

(A) includingを使うと「Brennen Claytonを含む」となり、前のthe world's leading experts on cyber security（サイバーセキュリティの世界一流の専門家たち）と上手くつながる。

☐ feature　動 〜を呼び物にする、出演させる
☐ leading　形 一流の

108.

Ms. Browning sold her house without the ------- of a real estate agent.

(A) support　協力、協力する
(B) supportive　協力的な
(C) supporting　supportの-ing形
(D) supported　supportの過去形・過去分詞

訳　Browningさんは、不動産業者の協力なしで彼女の家を売却した。

▶ 正解　(A)

前に冠詞the、後ろに前置詞ofがあるので、空所には名詞の(A) support（協力）が入る。without the support of a real estate agentで「不動産業者の協力なしで」という意味。(C) supportingも名詞的に使われることが可能だが、the supporting of a real estate agentでは「不動産業者への手助け」となり意味的に不適切。

☐ real estate　不動産

109.

After forty years ------- the Kendlewood Public Library, librarian Michael McConnell will be retiring on October 31.

(A) through　～を通り抜けて
(B) above　～の上に
(C) with　～に勤務して
(D) about　～に関して

訳　Kendlewood公立図書館に40年勤務して、司書のMichael McConnellは10月31日をもって退職する。

▶ 正解　(C)

(C) with には「～に勤務して」という意味があるので、これを使うと After forty years with the Kendlewood Public Library で「Kendlewood公立図書館に40年勤務して」となり、後の「10月31日をもって退職する」と上手くつながる。

□ librarian　名　司書
□ retire　動　退職する

110.

Five days before the workshop, the organization will start charging a fee for ------- registration.

(A) former　前の
(B) late　遅い
(C) behind　～の後ろに
(D) latter　後者の

訳　ワークショップの5日前から、団体は遅延登録料を請求し始める。

▶ 正解　(B)

料金請求の対象になるものを考えると、late registration（遅延登録）が適切。start charging a fee for late registration で「遅延登録料を請求し始める」という意味。

□ organization　名　団体
□ charge　動　（料金を）請求する
□ registration　名　登録

111.

Graphex design software has gone from being a tool for professionals to a program ------- can use.

(A) whenever　いつでも
(B) ourselves　私たち自身
(C) anyone　誰でも
(D) other　他の

訳　Graphexのデザインソフトは、プロ用のツールから誰でも使えるプログラムへと変わった。

▶ 正解　(C)

(C) anyone は「誰でも」という意味なので、これを使うと a program (that) anyone can use で「誰でも使えるプログラム」となり、文意に合う。(D) other は複数形の others であれば、「他の人たち」という意味になる。

□ go from A to B　AからBに変わる

112.

Montego Grill will be closed from 1:00 P.M. to 6:00 P.M. ------- a private function.

(A) along　～に沿って
(B) by　～のそばに
(C) from　～から
(D) for　～のために

訳　Montego Grillは、貸切りのイベントのため午後1時から6時まで閉店します。

▶ 正解　(D)

a private function は「貸切りのイベント」の意味。前置詞の (D) for は理由を示す働きがあるので、closed for a private function で「貸切りのイベントのため閉店する」となり、文意に合う。

□ closed　形　閉まった
□ function　名　催し、イベント

113.

Even though all the contestants were invited to the awards ceremony, only the winners were in -------.

(A) attended　attend（出席する）の過去形・過去分詞
(B) attendees　出席者（複数形）
(C) attending　attendの-ing形
(D) attendance　出席

訳　コンテストの参加者全員が授賞式に招待されていたにもかかわらず、受賞者だけが出席していた。

▶ 正解　(D)

be in attendanceで「出席している」の意味になるので、(D) attendance（出席）が正解。前置詞inが名詞attendanceを伴い、形容詞句として補語の役割をしている。

- even though　〜にもかかわらず
- contestant　名 コンテスト参加者
- invite　動 招待する

114.

If ------- pass is not activated, access to the building will be restricted to the main lobby.

(A) yourself　あなた自身
(B) yours　あなたのもの
(C) your　あなたの
(D) you　あなた

訳　もしあなたの入館証が有効になっていなければ、建物への出入りはメインロビーのみに制限されます。

▶ 正解　(C)

後ろに名詞のpass（入館証）があるので、(C) your（あなたの）を選ぶ。

- pass　名 入館証、出入許可証
- activate　動 有効にする
- access　名 出入り
- restrict　動 制限する

115.

The manager was impressed at how ------- the new salespeople are about the store's merchandise.

(A) knowledge　知識
(B) knowledgeable　知識が豊富な
(C) known　知られている
(D) knowingly　故意に

訳　マネージャーは、新しい販売員が店の商品についていかに知識が豊富かということに感心した。

▶ 正解　(B)

howは形容詞や副詞を伴いhow 〜 で「どれほど〜」という意味になる。この文では形容詞の(B) knowledgeable（知識が豊富な）を選ぶと、後ろに続く部分がthe new salespeople are knowledgeable about the store's merchandise.（新しい販売員は店の商品について知識が豊富である）となり、文が成り立つ。

- be impressed at 〜　〜に感銘を受ける
- merchandise　名 商品

116.

The factory owner released a statement confirming that an investigation into the ------- of the accident was underway.

(A) factor　要因
(B) control　制御
(C) opinion　意見
(D) cause　原因

訳　工場のオーナーは、事故の原因の調査が進行中であることを正式に発表する声明を出した。

▶ 正解　(D)

(D)を使うとthe cause of the accidentで「事故を引き起こした原因」となり文意に合う。

- release　動 発表する
- statement　名 声明
- confirm　動 正式に発表する
- investigation　名 調査
- underway　形 進行中で

117.

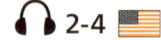

Richard Cooke and his team created the spectacular light show ------- for the Star-Pop concert tour.

(A) specify　特定する
(B) specifications　仕様、仕様書
(C) specifying　specifyの-ing形
(D) specifically　特別に

訳　Richard Cookeと彼のチームは、壮観なライトショーをStar-Popのコンサートツアーのために特別に作った。

▶ 正解　(D)

副詞の(D) specifically（特別に）を使うと、for 以下の前置詞句 for the Star-Pop concert tourを修飾する形になる（副詞は前置詞句を修飾する働きがある）。specifically for the Star-Pop concert tourで「Star-Popのコンサートツアーのために特別に」という意味になり、「壮観なライトショーを作った」という前半部分と上手くつながる。

☐ spectacular　形 壮観な

118.

A study by the Rialto Research Institute ------- that organic pesticides are more effective than their synthetic counterparts.

(A) told　～に伝えた
(B) brought　～を持ってきた
(C) found　～を見出した
(D) took　～を取った

訳　Rialto Research Instituteによる研究は、有機殺虫剤が合成殺虫剤より効果的であることを見出した。

▶ 正解　(C)

後ろに続くthat節で表されている内容は、研究結果からわかったことなので、(C) found（～を見出した）が正解。また、選択肢の他の動詞には、直後にthat節をとる用法はない。

☐ organic　形 有機の
☐ pesticide　名 殺虫剤
☐ synthetic　形 合成の
☐ counterpart　名 対応するもの（問題文では「殺虫剤」を受ける）

119.

Alana Shah was commissioned to design the memorial on the condition that ------- collaborate with another architect.

(A) she　彼女は
(B) hers　彼女のもの
(C) her　彼女の、彼女を
(D) herself　彼女自身

訳　Alana Shahは、別の建築家と共同で作業をするという条件で記念館の設計を依頼された。

▶ 正解　(A)

後ろに動詞のcollaborateが続いているので、文の主語として機能する(A) she（彼女は）を選ぶ。on the condition that（～という条件で）のthat節中では、動詞が原形になり、主語がsheでもcollaborateに三人称単数現在形のsが付かない（文法用語では仮定法現在と呼ばれる）。

☐ commission　動 依頼する
☐ memorial　名 記念館
☐ collaborate　動 共同で行う

120.

Seminar participants will be required to ------- a business plan that outlines the details of their proposed venture.

(A) developer　開発者
(B) develop　考案する
(C) development　発展
(D) developing　developの-ing形

訳　セミナーの参加者は、彼らが提案したベンチャー事業の詳細をまとめた事業計画を立案することが求められる。

▶ 正解　(B)

be required toは後ろに動詞の原形を伴い「～することが求められる」の意味を表す。よって、(B) developが正解。

☐ outline　動 概要を説明する
☐ propose　動 提案する
☐ venture　名 ベンチャー事業

121.

City council has introduced stringent maintenance requirements to improve the quality of ------- properties in Brownsville.

(A) renting　rentの-ing形
(B) rental　賃貸の
(C) rents　rentの三人称単数現在形、複数形
(D) rent　賃貸借する、賃借料

訳　市議会は、Brownsvilleの賃貸物件の質を向上させるために、厳重な保守管理義務を施行した。

▶ 正解　(B)

(B)を使うとrental propertiesで「賃貸物件」となり、文意に合う。また、rentalは「賃借、賃貸」という意味の名詞としても使われるので注意。

□ city council　市議会
□ introduce　動 施行する、導入する
□ stringent　形 厳格な
□ requirement　名 満たすべき義務

122.

A notice sent to Mr. Malone informed him that his vehicle ------- was set to expire on September 15.

(A) registration　登録
(B) registered　registerの過去形・過去分詞
(C) register　登録する
(D) registering　registerの-ing形

訳　Maloneさんに送られた通知は、車両登録が9月15日で期限切れになることを知らせた。

▶ 正解　(A)

(A)を使うとhis vehicle registrationで「彼の車両登録」という意味になり、後ろのwas set to expire (期限切れになる) と上手くつながる。

□ inform　動 知らせる
□ registration　名 登録
□ be set to ～　～することになっている
□ expire　動 期限が切れる

123.

Although Ms. Robinson took a taxi from the airport, she usually ------- for the company limousine to pick her up.

(A) decides　決める
(B) arranges　手配する
(C) contacts　～に連絡する
(D) expects　～を期待する

訳　Robinsonさんは空港からタクシーに乗ったが、普段は会社のリムジンが迎えに来るよう手配する。

▶ 正解　(B)

「通常～しているのに（今回は）タクシーに乗った」という文意をふまえて(B) arranges (手配する) を選ぶ。arrange for ～は「～を手配する、準備する」という成句。forの後がthe company limousine (会社のリムジン) であるから、他の選択肢では文意に合わない。

□ pick up　迎えに行く

124.

------- the heavy snowfall, Ms. McFarland set up a conference call with the client instead of driving to his office.

(A) Whether　～かどうか
(B) Given　～を考慮して
(C) As of　～現在
(D) Except for　～を除いて

訳　大雪を考慮して、McFarlandさんは、顧客のオフィスまで車で行く代わりに彼と電話会議をする手はずを整えた。

▶ 正解　(B)

Givenは前置詞として「～を考慮して」の意味を持つ。Given the heavy snowfallで「大雪を考慮して」となり、「車で行く代わりに電話会議をする手はずを整えた」と上手くつながる。

□ set up　手はずを整える
□ conference call　電話会議

125. 🎧 2-5 🇬🇧

The redevelopment plan includes building a park between Fillmore Road and Blackridge Street, ------- an orchard is currently located.

(A) where　～する場所（場所を受ける関係詞）
(B) what　～するもの（先行詞＋whichの機能をする関係詞）
(C) when　～する時（時を受ける関係詞）
(D) which　～するもの（物を受ける関係詞）

訳　再開発計画は、現在は果樹園があるFillmore RoadとBlackridge Streetの間に公園を作ることを含んでいる。

▶ 正解　(A)

文意からカンマ以下はAn orchard is currently located between Fillmore Road and Blackridge Street.（果樹園は現在、Fillmore RoadとBlackridge Streetの間にある）の意味になることがわかる。(A) whereはbetween Fillmore Road and Blackridge Streetのように前置詞＋名詞で示されている場所を受ける働きをする。

□ redevelopment　名 再開発
□ orchard　名 果樹園
□ be located　位置する

126. 🎧 2-6 🇬🇧

Although the committee has met twice to address the dispute, the members still remain ------- over the issue.

(A) attentive　注意している
(B) divided　分かれている
(C) devoted　献身的な
(D) opposite　反対の

訳　委員会は論争に対処すべく2度会合を持ったが、委員はその問題をめぐりまだ意見が分かれたままである。

▶ 正解　(B)

動詞remainは、後ろに形容詞を伴い「～のままである」という意味を表す。the members still remain divided over the issue.とすると「委員はその問題をめぐりまだ意見が分かれたままである」となり、前半部分と上手くつながる。divideの後ろで何に関して意見が分かれているか示す場合、前置詞overを使う。

□ meet　動 会合を持つ
□ address　動 取り組む
□ dispute　名 論争

127. 🎧 2-6 🇺🇸

Once the plant is ------- operational, it will produce more than fifty thousand bottles per day.

(A) adversely　逆に
(B) shortly　まもなく
(C) fully　完全に
(D) carefully　慎重に

訳　工場が完全に稼働できる状態になると、1日あたり5万本以上の瓶を生産することになる。

▶ 正解　(C)

選択肢は全て副詞であるから「工場が～に稼働できる状態になると」という文意に合うものを選ぶ。(C) fully（完全に）を使えば、Once the plant is fully operationalで「工場が完全に稼働できる状態になると」となり意味が通る。

□ once　接 ～すると
□ operational　形 稼働できる状態の
□ produce　動 生産する

128.

The number of visitors to the island is expected ------- significantly after the ferry's service hours are extended.

(A) increased　increase（増える）の過去形・過去分詞
(B) increases　increaseの三人称単数現在形
(C) increasingly　ますます
(D) to increase　increaseのto不定詞

訳　フェリーの運航時間が延長された後には、島を訪れる人の数は大幅に増えると予想されている。

▶ 正解　(D)

動詞expectは「期待する、予期する」を意味し、be expected to～で「～することが予想される」となる。(D) to increaseを選ぶと、The number of visitors to the island is expected to increase significantlyで「島を訪れる人の数は大幅に増えると予想されている」となり意味が通る。

□ significantly　副 大幅に
□ service hours　運航時間
□ extend　動 延長する

129.

According to *Bizsphere Magazine*, Aerowflight is now ------- the world's ten largest aircraft manufacturers.

(A) among　～の中の1つ
(B) unless　～でない限り
(C) against　～に対して
(D) until　～まで

訳　*Bizsphere Magazine*によれば、Aerowflightは今や世界の10大航空機製造会社の1つである。

▶ 正解　(A)

前がAerowflight is now（Aerowflightは今や）、後ろがthe world's ten largest aircraft manufacturers（世界の10大航空機製造会社）なので、(A) amongを選ぶと「Aerowflightは今や世界の10大航空機製造会社の1つである」となり意味が通る。この場合の前置詞amongは「～の中の1つ」という意味になる。

□ according to ～　～によると
□ the world's ten largest　世界の10大～

130.

The CEO acted on the ------- of the finance committee to make more investments.

(A) association　協会
(B) progression　進歩
(C) development　開発
(D) recommendation　提言

訳　CEOは、より多くの投資を行うという財務委員会の提言に従って行動した。

▶ 正解　(D)

act onは「（忠告、情報などに）従って行動する」の意味。(D)を選び、the recommendation of the finance committeeとすると、「財務委員会の提言」となり前のThe CEO acted on（CEOは～に従って行動した）と上手くつながる。

□ finance　名 財務
□ committee　名 委員会
□ investment　名 投資

Part 6 解答・解説

Questions 131–134 refer to the following e-mail. 🎧 2-7 🇬🇧

To: nbrowning@ynrgtech.com
From: ktaylor@xylosystems.com
Date: February 19
Subject: Reference Request

Dear Mr. Browning:

A former employee of your company, Nancy Burroughs, has ------- **131.** for a position with our organization. She provided your name and your e-mail address as a reference. As part of our recruiting process, I am writing to ask if you would be willing ------- **132.** some information about her.

------- **133.**. This outlines the duties of the post that Ms. Burroughs has applied for. I would be grateful if you would comment on her ------- **134.** for the post. Any other details you can add would be greatly appreciated.

Thank you.

Kathleen Taylor
Personnel Director
Xylo Systems

問題131～134は次のEメールに関するものです。

宛先　：　nbrowning@ynrgtech.com
送信者　：　ktaylor@xylosystems.com
日付　：　2月19日
件名　：　照会の要請

Browning様

貴社の元社員であるNancy Burroughsが弊社の職に応募しています。彼女は、照会先としてあなたの名前とEメールアドレスを提供しました。弊社の新人採用過程の一環として、あなたが彼女に関する情報を共有していただけるかお伺いするため、ご連絡しております。

職務記述書がこのEメールに添付されています。これは、Burroughsさんが応募した職の責務の概要を示しています。同職への彼女の適性についてご意見をいただければ幸いです。その他、どんな細かい事でも加えていただければ、大変ありがたく存じます。

ありがとうございます。

Kathleen Taylor
人事部長
Xylo Systems

☐ **provide** 動 提供する　　☐ **reference** 名 照会先　　☐ **recruit** 動 採用する
☐ **outline** 動 概要を示す　　☐ **duty** 名 責務　　☐ **grateful** 形 感謝している
☐ **appreciate** 動 感謝する

131.

(A) accepted　受け入れた
(B) applied　申し込んだ
(C) filled　満たした
(D) offered　申し出た

▶ **正解　(B)**

後ろにfor a position with our organization（弊社の職に）とあるので、(B) applied（申し込んだ）が適切。has applied for a positionで「職に応募している」となり、照会先に職への適性を尋ねている文脈に合う。

132.

(A) of sharing　of + share（共有する）の -ing形
(B) to share　shareのto不定詞
(C) shared　shareの過去形・過去分詞
(D) to have shared　shareの不定詞の完了形

▶ **正解　(B)**

willingはto不定詞を伴いbe willing to 〜で「〜することをいとわない」という意味になる。(B) to shareを使うと、be willing to shareで「共有することをいとわない」となり、文意にも合う。不定詞の完了形の(D) to have sharedは、過去のことを表す形なので不適切。

133.

(A) It will be useful in making a hiring decision.
　　それは、採用の決定をする際に役立ちます。
(B) For example, you can ask about her role.
　　例えば、あなたは彼女の役割について尋ねることができます。
(C) We would like a response by February 25.
　　2月25日までにご返答をいただきたく存じます。
(D) A job description is attached to this e-mail.
　　職務記述書がこのEメールに添付されています。

▶ **正解　(D)**

後ろのThis outlines the duties of the post that Ms. Burroughs has applied for.（これは、Burroughsさんが応募した職の責務の概要を示しています）のThisは、前に出てきたものを受けるので、(D)を選ぶとThis がA job description（職務記述書）を受けることになり、意味が通る。

☐ **decision**　名 決定
☐ **response**　名 返答

134.

(A) suitable　適切な
(B) suited　適した
(C) suitably　適切に
(D) suitability　適性

▶ **正解　(D)**

前にher、後ろに前置詞forがあるので、空所には名詞が入る。選択肢中、名詞は(D) suitability（適性）のみで、これを使うとher suitability for the postで「職への彼女の適性」の意味になる。

Questions 135–138 refer to the following notice.

You are invited to join our new book club. We will be discussing contemporary works of fiction twice a month. Our kick-off meeting will take place at the Brentwood Library on September 28. ------- (135.) meetings will be held on the second and fourth Thursday of every month at 7:00 P.M.

The first novel we will be reading is *Fleeting Twilight* by Amos Ballard. ------- (136.). The book is currently available in most bookstores.

------- (137.) you are interested in becoming a member of the Brentwood Library Book Club, e-mail Elton Kesey at ekesey@btdlibrary.org. Please let him know that you are coming ------- (138.) enough chairs and tables can be set up ahead of time.

問題135〜138は次のお知らせに関するものです。

私たちの新しい読書クラブへのご入会をお勧めいたします。私たちは、月に2回、小説の現代作品について語り合う予定です。発足会は、9月28日にBrentwood Libraryで行われます。それ以降の会合は、毎月第2、第4木曜日の午後7時に行われます。

私たちが読む最初の小説は、Amos Ballardの『Fleeting Twilight』です。参加者は事前にそれを読んでおいてください。同書は、現在ほとんどの書店で購入可能です。

もしBrentwood Library Book Clubの会員になることに関心があれば、ekesey@btdlibrary.orgにElton Kesey宛てにEメールをお送りください。十分な椅子とテーブルを事前に用意できるように、あなたが来ることを彼にお知らせください。

- □ **invite** 動 勧める　□ **discuss** 動 意見を交わす　□ **contemporary** 形 現代の
- □ **kick-off meeting** 発足会　□ **take place** 行われる　□ **be held** 催される
- □ **currently** 副 現在　□ **available** 形 手に入る

135.

(A) Constant 絶え間ない
(B) Repetitive 繰り返しの
(C) Consecutive 連続した
(D) Subsequent 後に続く

▶ 正解 (D)

前の文ではOur kick-off meeting（発足会）が9月28日に行われることが述べられており、後ろにmeetings will be held on the second and fourth Thursday of every month at 7:00 P.M.（会合は、毎月第2、第4木曜日の午後7時に行われます）とあるので、空所には発足会の後の会合であることを示す(D) Subsequentが適切。Subsequent meetingsで「それ以降の会合」の意味。

136.

(A) He did attend our previous meeting.
　　彼は、私たちの前の会合に確かに出席しました。
(B) It will be released on October 20.
　　それは10月20日に発売になります。
(C) Participants should read it in advance.
　　参加者は事前にそれを読んでおいてください。
(D) However, the library is closed on Monday.
　　しかし、図書館は月曜日が休館日です。

▶ 正解 (C)

前の文で初めの会合で取り上げる小説が示されており、後ろの文ではその小説が書店で購入可能であることが述べられている。前後に課題小説に関する文があるので、(C)を使うと、itがその小説を受けて、「事前にその小説を読んでおくこと」という意味になり、文意に合う。

□ previous 形 前の
□ release 動 発売する
□ participant 名 参加者
□ in advance 事前に

137.

(A) For ～のために
(B) Until ～する時まで
(C) If もし
(D) While ～の間に

▶ 正解 (C)

(C) Ifを使いIf you are interested in becoming a member（もし会員になることに関心があれば）とすると、後ろのe-mail Elton Kesey at ekesey@btdlibrary.org.（ekesey@btdlibrary.orgにElton Kesey宛てにEメールをお送りください）と上手くつながる。

138.

(A) in case 念のため～に備えて
(B) so that ～できるように
(C) whereas ～である一方で
(D) although ～ではあるが

▶ 正解 (B)

(B) so thatは目的を表す節を導くので、so that enough chairs and tables can be set up ahead of time. で「十分な椅子とテーブルを事前に用意できるように」となり、前のPlease let him know that you are coming（あなたが来ることを彼にお知らせください）と上手くつながる。

Questions 139–142 refer to the following information.

Preordering Transgaia Meals

Transgaia Airways understands that more control over the inflight dining experience is what passengers want. That is ------- we offer the convenience of selecting a meal in advance of flights.
139.

Simply enter your flight booking code on the reservations section of this Web site and then choose the meal option of your -------. Meals can be ordered between ten days and twenty-four hours prior to departure. Confirmation of the selection ------- by e-mail.
140. **141.**

If you have a particular dietary requirement, please let us know. -------. All you have to do is contact your travel consultant or the Transgaia Reservations Office with the special meal request.
142.

問題139〜142は次の情報に関するものです。

Transgaiaの機内食事前注文

Transgaia Airwaysは、乗客の皆様が機内でのお食事に関して高い自由度を求めていると理解しています。それが、当社が飛行に先立ってお食事を選ぶ便宜を提供する理由です。

このウェブサイトの予約の欄にあなたの航空券予約コードを入力して、それからお好みの機内食オプションを選択するだけです。お食事は、出発の10日前から24時間前までの間でご注文いただけます。お選びになったお食事の確認はEメールで送られます。

もし特別な食事制限がございましたらお知らせください。適切な代わりのお食事をご提供することが可能です。旅行代理店のスタッフまたはTransgaia Reservations Officeまで、特別機内食申込みのご連絡をいただくだけで手配いたします。

- inflight 形 機内の
- dining 名 食事
- offer 動 提供する
- convenience 名 便宜
- in advance of 〜 〜に先立ち
- enter 動 入力する
- prior to 〜 〜の前に
- departure 名 出発
- confirmation 名 確認
- particular 形 特別な
- dietary requirement 食事制限

139.

(A) why　理由を示す関係詞
(B) what　事柄を示す関係詞
(C) where　場所を示す関係詞
(D) who　人を示す関係詞

▶ **正解　(A)**

前の文が後ろの we offer the convenience of selecting a meal in advance of flights.（当社が飛行に先立ってお食事を選ぶ便宜を提供する）の理由になっているので、(A) why が正解。That is why ～で「それが～の理由です」の意味。

140.

(A) preference　好み
(B) preferable　好ましい
(C) preferring　prefer（～をより好む）の -ing 形
(D) preferred　prefer の過去形・過去分詞

▶ **正解　(A)**

前に your があり、後ろに続く語がないので、空所には名詞が入る。選択肢中、名詞は (A) preference（好み）で、これを使うと the meal option of your preference で「あなたのお好みの機内食オプション」の意味になる。

141.

(A) sends　send（送る）の三人称単数現在形
(B) was sent　send の受動態の過去形
(C) will be sent　will + be sent（受動態）
(D) is sending　send の現在進行形

▶ **正解　(C)**

主語の Confirmation of the selection（選んだ物の確認）は「送られる」ものであるので、動詞 send との間には受動の関係が成り立つ。また、確認が送られるのは、好みの機内食をウェブサイト上で選択した後なので、未来のことを表す (C) will be sent（送られる）が正解。

142.

(A) However, another return flight might not be available.
　しかし、別の帰りの便は利用できないことがあります。
(B) We can provide you with a suitable alternative meal.
　適切な代わりのお食事をご提供することが可能です。
(C) There are several procedures you need to follow first.
　まず、ふまえていただく必要のある手順がいくつかございます。
(D) One will be sent to you soon after we are informed.
　こちらに連絡が入り次第、あなたに1つお送りいたします。

▶ **正解　(B)**

前に If you have a particular dietary requirement, please let us know.（もし特別な食事制限がございましたらお知らせください）とあるので、(B) We can provide you with a suitable alternative meal.（適切な代わりのお食事をご提供することが可能です）とすると上手くつながる。

- alternative　形 代わりの
- procedure　名 手続き
- follow　動 ふまえる
- inform　動 知らせる

Questions 143–146 refer to the following letter.

Mr. Yun Huan
Aggentek Engineering Ltd.
2477 Minyou Road,
Hsinchu, Taiwan

Dear Mr. Huan:

Clarsight Films has been making photographic films for sixty-two years. In the wake of the digital photography age, however, the company recognized a need to diversify. Therefore, ------- **143.** digital cameras quickly replaced film cameras, we expanded our expertise to other industries.

In a move to represent all of our products and services accurately, we will change our name to Clarsight Technologies. ------- **144.** . We would appreciate it if you would bring this to the attention of your accounts department and change your records ------- **145.** .

We want to assure you that with our new name we will continue to deliver the same high level of quality you have come ------- **146.** from us. And we look forward to continuing our business relationship with you.

Sincerely,

Gareth Donovan
President, Clarsight Films

問題143〜146は次の手紙に関するものです。

Yun Huan様
Aggentek Engineering Ltd.
2477 Minyou Road,
Hsinchu, Taiwan

Huan様

Clarsight Filmsは、62年間写真用フィルムを作ってきましたが、デジタル写真時代の到来を受けて、多様化の必要性を認識いたしました。従って、デジタルカメラが急速にフィルムカメラに取って代わった一方で、私たちは専門技術を他の産業へ広げていきました。

私たちの全ての製品とサービスを正確に表す1つの策として、社名をClarsight Technologiesに変更いたします。この変更は、3月1日に有効になります。これを貴社の経理部へ知らせて、それに応じて記録を変更していただければ幸いです。

新しい社名になりましても、貴社が私たちに期待するようになられたこれまでと同じ高水準の品質をお届けし続けることをお約束いたします。そして、貴社との取引関係を続けていくことを楽しみにしております。

敬具

Gareth Donovan
Clarsight Films 社長

Part 6 | 解答・解説

- □ in the wake of ～　～を受けて
- □ recognize 　動 認識する
- □ diversify 　動 多様化する
- □ replace 　動 取って代わる
- □ expand 　動 広げる
- □ expertise 　名 専門技術
- □ in a move to ～　～する策として
- □ represent 　動 表す
- □ accurately 　副 正確に
- □ appreciate 　動 感謝する
- □ assure 　動 保証する

143.

(A) while　～する一方で
(B) as if　～するかのように
(C) except　～を除いて
(D) unless　～でない限り

▶ 正解　(A)

後ろの digital cameras quickly replaced film cameras とそれに続く we expanded our expertise to other industries. の関係を考えると、「デジタルカメラが急速にフィルムカメラに取って代わった」と「私たちは専門技術を他の産業へ広げた」の2つの事柄が対比させられる形で並べられているので、(A) while（～する一方で）が適切。while は「～の間」という意味の用法だけでなく、このように対比関係を示すこともできる。

144.

(A) You are welcome to attend this special event.
この特別イベントへのあなたのご出席を歓迎します。
(B) The relocation will not impact our partnership.
移転は、私たちの取引関係に影響いたしません。
(C) Please be aware that these are being revised.
これらは修正中ですのでご注意ください。
(D) The change will become effective on March 1.
この変更は、3月1日に有効になります。

▶ 正解　(D)

前の文で社名が変更になることが伝えられているので、(D) The change will become effective on March 1.（この変更は、3月1日に有効になります）を選ぶと、The change が社名の変更を受けることになり、上手くつながる。

- □ relocation 　名 移転
- □ impact 　動 影響を与える
- □ revise 　動 修正する

145.

(A) accordingly　それに応じて
(B) suddenly　突然
(C) practically　ほとんど、実際に
(D) regularly　定期的に

▶ 正解　(A)

(A) accordingly（それに応じて）を使うと、change your records accordingly で「それに応じて記録を変更する（＝社名が変わるのでそれに合う形で記録を変更する）」となり、社名の変更に伴う情報の更新を依頼している文脈に合う。

146.

(A) expectation　期待
(B) expected　expect（～を期待する）の過去形・過去分詞
(C) to expect　expect の to 不定詞
(D) expectantly　期待して

▶ 正解　(C)

come は、後ろに to 不定詞を伴い「～するようになる」という意味を表すので、(C)を使うと have come to expect で「期待するようになった」となり、上手くつながる。空所を含む文では quality の後ろに関係代名詞の that が省略されており、the same high level of quality (that) you have come to expect from us で「貴社が私たちに期待するようになられたこれまでと同じ高水準の品質」という意味になる。

121

Part 7　解答・解説

Questions 147–148 refer to the following announcement.

1文書：お知らせ　　　🎧 2-11 🇬🇧

Date: January 12

Announcement for all Sales and Service Staff

Effective February 1, Thomas Salvatore will assume the duties of floor manager at our customer call center in Virginia. He is currently a sales team supervisor at our Kentucky branch, where his assistant, Rita Cockrell, will be taking over his position when he leaves.

Mr. Salvatore has worked at Vastynet for eleven years. Prior to serving as a branch supervisor, he was a member of the project team that introduced our new broadband services in Pennsylvania. His first job with the company was service technician at our Delaware location.

We are very pleased to announce this promotion, and we are confident that Mr. Salvatore will demonstrate effective leadership in his new role.

問題147〜148は次のお知らせに関するものです。

日付：1月12日

販売・サービススタッフへのお知らせ

2月1日付けで、Thomas Salvatoreが、Virginiaの顧客コールセンターのフロアマネージャーの職に就きます。現在、彼はKentucky支社の営業チームの主任で、そこを離れる時に、彼のアシスタントのRita Cockrellがその職を引き継ぐことになっています。

Salvatoreさんは、Vastynetで11年間働いています。支社の主任を務める前は、Pennsylvaniaで新規ブロードバンドサービスを売り出したプロジェクトチームの一員でした。当社における最初の職は、Delaware支社でのサービス技術者でした。

我々はこの昇進を発表できることを非常に喜ばしく思っており、またSalvatoreさんが新しい役職においても効果的なリーダーシップを示してくれることを確信しております。

- ☐ **effective** +〈日付〉 〜付けで
- ☐ **assume** 動 (役割などを) 担う
- ☐ **duty** 名 職務
- ☐ **supervisor** 名 主任、監督者
- ☐ **take over** 引き継ぐ
- ☐ **position** 名 役職
- ☐ **prior to 〜** 〜の前は
- ☐ **introduce** 動 売り出す
- ☐ **be pleased to 〜** 喜んで〜する
- ☐ **promotion** 名 昇進
- ☐ **confident** 形 自信がある
- ☐ **demonstrate** 動 示す
- ☐ **effective** 形 効果的な
- ☐ **role** 名 役割

147.

🎧 2-11 🇺🇸

What is the main purpose of the announcement?
(A) To encourage staff participation
(B) To promote some new services
(C) To announce a personnel change
(D) To introduce some job openings

お知らせの主な目的は何ですか。
(A) 職員の参加を促すこと
(B) 新しいサービスを宣伝すること
(C) 人事異動を発表すること
(D) 求人を紹介すること

▶ 正解 (C)

冒頭のEffective February 1, Thomas Salvatore will assume the duties of floor manager at our customer call center in Virginia.（2月1日付けで、Thomas Salvatoreが、Virginiaの顧客コールセンターのフロアマネージャーの職に就きます）や、最後のWe are very pleased to announce this promotion（我々はこの昇進を発表できることを非常に喜ばしく思っており）から、(C)が正解であるとわかる。

□ encourage 動 促す
□ promote 動 宣伝する
□ job opening 求人、就職口

▶ 言い換えポイント   promotion ➡ personnel change

148.

🎧 2-11 🇺🇸

Where does Mr. Salvatore work now?
(A) In Virginia
(B) In Kentucky
(C) In Pennsylvania
(D) In Delaware

Salvatoreさんは、現在どこで働いていますか。
(A) Virginiaで
(B) Kentuckyで
(C) Pennsylvaniaで
(D) Delawareで

▶ 正解 (B)

He is currently a sales team supervisor at our Kentucky branch（現在、彼はKentucky支社の営業チームの主任で）より、Salvatoreさんが現在Kentuckyで働いていることがわかる。

Questions 149–150 refer to the following text message chain.

1文書：テキストメッセージ

🎧 2-12 🇬🇧 🇺🇸

Wanda Hess   12:39 P.M.
Have you left the building already, Marcus? I see the red folder on your desk. Inside are the blueprints I prepared for you, right? I thought you were going to bring them to your meeting at ORT Construction.

Marcus Naylor   12:42 P.M.
You're right. I forgot them. It's not a big deal, though. ORT has a copy. But I was hoping to show them the new dimensions I wrote down on the second page.

Wanda Hess   12:43 P.M.
I could fax that one to someone at ORT.

Marcus Naylor   12:44 P.M.
Actually, could you take pictures of the notes with your phone and send them to me?

Wanda Hess   12:46 P.M.
Sure, I'll do that now. See you when you get back to the office.

問題149〜150は次のテキストメッセージのやりとりに関するものです。

Wanda Hess   ［午後12時39分］
すでに建物を出ましたか、Marcus。あなたの机の上に赤いフォルダーがあります。中にあるのは、私があなたのために用意した設計図ですよね。あなたがORT Constructionでのミーティングに持っていくのだと思っていましたが。

Marcus Naylor   ［午後12時42分］
その通りです。忘れてしまいました。でも、大したことではありません。ORTは、コピーを持っていますので。しかし、2ページ目に書き込んだ新しい寸法を彼らに見せたいと思っていました。

Wanda Hess   ［午後12時43分］
私がORTの誰か宛てにファックスしましょうか。

Marcus Naylor   ［午後12時44分］
それより、携帯電話でメモの写真を撮って、私に送ってもらえませんか。

Wanda Hess   ［午後12時46分］
わかりました、今、送ります。では、後ほどオフィスで。

☐ **blueprint** 名 設計図   ☐ **dimension** 名 寸法

149.

At 12:42 P.M., what does Mr. Naylor mean when he writes, "It's not a big deal"?
(A) A meeting is not important.
(B) A contract is not large.
(C) A mistake is not serious.
(D) An agreement is not significant.

午後12時42分に、Naylorさんが書いている"It's not a big deal"は、何を意味していますか。
(A) 会議は重要ではない。
(B) 契約は大きくない。
(C) ミスは深刻ではない。
(D) 合意は重要ではない。

▶ **正解** (C)

Naylorさんは、設計図を忘れたことに対してIt's not a big deal（大したことではありません）と言っている。「設計図を忘れたこと」はmistake（ミス）にあたるので、(C) A mistake is not serious.（ミスは深刻ではない）が正解。

☐ **contract** 名 契約
☐ **serious** 形 深刻な
☐ **agreement** 名 合意
☐ **significant** 形 重要な

▶ 言い換えポイント   not a big deal ➡ not serious

150.

What does Mr. Naylor ask Ms. Hess to do?
(A) Revise some figures
(B) Send some photographs
(C) Fax a document
(D) Call a client

Naylorさんは、Hessさんに何をするよう頼んでいますか。
(A) 数字を訂正する
(B) 何枚かの写真を送る
(C) 書類をファックスする
(D) 顧客に電話をかける

▶ **正解** (B)

午後12時43分の「書類をファックスしましょうか」というHessさんの申し出に対して、Naylorさんはcould you take pictures of the notes with your phone and send them to me?（携帯電話でメモの写真を撮って、私に送ってもらえませんか）と頼んでいるので、(B) Send some photographs（何枚かの写真を送る）が正解。

☐ **revise** 動 訂正する
☐ **figure** 名 数字
☐ **client** 名 顧客

Questions 151–152 refer to the following notice.

1文書：告知　　　🎧 2-13 🇬🇧

Tuesday Morning Delays

Traks Transit would like to apologize for the disruptions and delays that occurred during morning commute hours on Tuesday, August 26. Service was suspended due to a signal failure caused by an electrical problem on our West District Line. We offered passengers complimentary tickets for subway and bus routes connecting Glendale to the downtown area. Service was restored by 11:10 A.M.

We sincerely apologize for the inconvenience and appreciate your understanding in this matter.

問題151〜152は次の告知に関するものです。

火曜日午前の遅延

Traks Transitは、8月26日火曜日の朝の通勤時間帯に発生した運休と遅延についてお詫び申し上げます。West District Lineでの電気的な問題に起因する信号機故障のために、サービスが一時停止しました。乗客の皆様にはGlendaleと市の中心部をつなぐ地下鉄とバス路線の無料切符をご用意いたしました。サービスは午前11時10分までに復旧いたしました。

ご不便を心からお詫びすると共に、この問題に対するご理解に感謝いたします。

- ☐ **apologize** 動 謝罪する　☐ **disruption** 名 途切れること　☐ **delay** 名 遅延
- ☐ **occur** 動 起こる　☐ **commute** 名 通勤　☐ **suspend** 動 一時的に止める
- ☐ **failure** 名 故障　☐ **cause** 動 引き起こす　☐ **complimentary** 形 無料の
- ☐ **connect** 動 つなぐ　☐ **restore** 動 復旧させる　☐ **inconvenience** 名 不便
- ☐ **appreciate** 動 感謝する

151.

Where would the notice most likely appear?
(A) In a bus terminal
(B) In a travel agency
(C) In a train station
(D) In a convenience store

告知はおそらくどこに掲示されますか。
(A) バスターミナルに
(B) 旅行代理店に
(C) 鉄道の駅に
(D) コンビニエンスストアに

▶ **正解** (C)

morning commute hours（朝の通勤時間帯）やa signal failure（信号機故障）、さらにはWe offered passengers complimentary tickets（乗客の皆様には無料切符をご用意いたしました）などから、(C) In a train station（鉄道の駅に）であると判断できる。

152.

What is explained in the notice?
(A) How a device was fixed
(B) Where to get a refund
(C) When a bus departs
(D) Why a service stopped

告知では、何が説明されていますか。
(A) 機器が修理された方法
(B) 払い戻しを受ける場所
(C) バスが出発する時刻
(D) サービスが止まった理由

▶ **正解** (D)

Service was suspended due to a signal failure caused by an electrical problem on our West District Line.（West District Lineでの電気的な問題に起因する信号機故障のために、サービスが一時停止しました）でサービスが止まった理由が説明されている。

- **device** 名 機器
- **refund** 名 払い戻し
- **depart** 動 出発する

Questions 153–154 refer to the following letter.

MEADOWS PUBLIC LIBRARY
7644 Apache Drive, Jonesboro, AR 72401

September 29

Timothy Zhang
6438 Access Road
Jonesboro, AR 72397

Dear Mr. Zhang:

The items listed below are overdue. Both of the books should have been returned to the library by September 15. Please bring them to our circulation counter and pay the applicable charges at your earliest convenience.

If you have already brought the items back to the library, we request that you call the Circulation Department at 555-7985 to inform us of the situation.

Thank you in advance for your cooperation.

Circulation Department
Meadows Public Library

Library card holder: Timothy Zhang
Library ID: PIUJDF 995835
Accrued fines (to date): $5.60

Title	Learn to Do Your Own Programming
Author	Hubert A. Murray
Publisher	Bollinger-Austin Press
Title	A Beginner's Guide to Computer Programming
Author	Erik Forester
Publisher	Percipient Publishing Ltd.

問題153〜154は次の手紙に関するものです。

Meadows公立図書館
7644 Apache Drive, Jonesboro, AR 72401

9月29日

Timothy Zhang
6438 Access Road
Jonesboro, AR 72397

Zhang様

下記に挙げた品目は返却期限が過ぎています。2冊とも9月15日までに返却されなければなりませんでした。なるべく早く、それらを貸出返却カウンターにお持ちになり、適用される延滞料をお支払いください。

もしすでに下記品目を図書館に返却されている場合は、555-7985の貸出返却部にお電話いただき、その旨お伝えいただけますようお願いいたします。

ご協力いただきありがとうございます。

貸出返却部
Meadows公立図書館

図書館カード所有者：Timothy Zhang
図書館ID：PIUJDF995835
累積延滞料（本日まで）：5ドル60セント

書名：『Learn to Do Your Own Programming』
著者：Hubert A. Murray
出版社：Bollinger-Austin Press

書名：『A Beginner's Guide to Computer Programming』
著者：Erik Forester
出版社：Percipient Publishing Ltd.

- □ list 動 挙げる
- □ overdue 形 期限の過ぎた
- □ circulation counter 貸出返却カウンター
- □ applicable 形 適用される
- □ charge 名 料金
- □ inform 動 知らせる
- □ accrue 動 生じる
- □ fine 名 罰金、延滞料

153.

2-14

Why did the library send the letter to Mr. Zhang?
(A) To inform him that books may be picked up
(B) To thank him for making a payment
(C) To request that he return some books
(D) To remind him to renew his library card

なぜ図書館はZhangさんに手紙を送りましたか。
(A) 本を受け取れると知らせるため
(B) 支払いに対して礼を述べるため
(C) 本を返却するように要請するため
(D) 図書館カードを更新するよう再度知らせるため

▶ 正解 (C)

冒頭で返却期限が過ぎている図書があることが伝えられ、出来るだけ早い返却が求められている。よって、(C)が正解。

- □ pick up 受け取る
- □ make a payment 支払いをする
- □ return 動 返却する
- □ remind 動 思い出させる

154.

2-14

What can be inferred from the letter?
(A) The library card is enclosed.
(B) The subject of the books is the same.
(C) The library has two branches.
(D) The books were written by the same author.

手紙から何が推測されますか。
(A) 図書館カードが同封されている。
(B) 本のテーマが同じである。
(C) 図書館には2つの館がある。
(D) 本は同じ著者によって書かれた。

▶ 正解 (B)

手紙の終わりに挙げられている2冊の本のタイトルは *Learn to Do Your Own Programming* と *A Beginner's Guide to Computer Programming* となっており、共にプログラミングに関するものであると推測できるので、テーマが同じであると言える。よって、(B)が正解。

- □ enclose 動 同封する

Questions 155–157 refer to the following receipt.

1文書：レシート

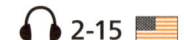

🎧 2-15 🇺🇸

```
              Ratcliff & Sons
              3420 Hillcrest Road
              Minneapolis, MN 55401
                  555-7257

    September 18 (3:02 P.M.)
    Transaction: 24558
    Payment method: OVC Credit Card

    Lime Green Latex Paint        $36.70
    Cordless Drill                $73.68
    Hammer                        $19.99
    Paint Roller                  $28.25
    Subtotal                     $158.62
    Sales Tax                     $12.33
    Total                        $170.95


    ───────── Bob O'Neil ─────────
            Cardholder Signature

    All return items must be accompanied by a
    sales receipt and brought back to the store
    within 30 days of purchase. Only items that
    are returned in an unused condition and in
    their original packaging can be accepted.
    Please be aware that all paints and paint-
    related products, except for rollers, are
    non-refundable and cannot be returned to the
    store for exchange or store credit. Defective
    electronic devices may be returned for a
    refund, exchange, or store credit.

              CUSTOMER COPY
```

問題155〜157は次のレシートに関するものです。

Ratcliff & Sons
3420 Hillcrest Road
Minneapolis, MN 55401
555-7257

9月18日（午後3時02分）
取引番号：24558
支払い方法：OVC クレジットカード

ライムグリーンラテックス塗料	36ドル70セント
コードレスドリル	73ドル68セント
ハンマー	19ドル99セント
塗装用ローラー	28ドル25セント
小計	158ドル62セント
消費税	12ドル33セント
合計	170ドル95セント

Bob O'Neil

カード所有者の署名

全ての返品商品はレシートを添えて、購入から30日以内に店に戻されなければなりません。未使用の状態で元の梱包に入った品物に限り、返品を受け付けます。ローラーを除く、全ての塗料と塗装関連製品は、返金不可で交換やストアクレジットによる返品をお受けできないことをご留意ください。欠陥のある電子機器の返品は、返金、交換、ストアクレジットのいずれかでご対応いたします。

顧客用コピー

- □ **return item** 返品商品　　□ **accompany** 動 伴う　　□ **purchase** 名 購入
- □ **return** 動 返品する　　□ **unused** 形 未使用の　　□ **packaging** 名 梱包
- □ **accept** 動 受け付ける　　□ **non-refundable** 形 返金不可の
- □ **store credit** ストアクレジット（返品した品物と同額分の買い物ができる金券）
- □ **defective** 形 欠陥のある　　□ **refund** 名 払い戻し

🎧 2-15 🇬🇧

155.

Where was the receipt most likely issued?
(A) At a delivery company
(B) At a hardware store
(C) At a post office
(D) At a painting company

レシートはおそらくどこで発行されましたか。
(A) 運送会社で
(B) ホームセンターで
(C) 郵便局で
(D) 塗装会社で

▶ 正解　(B)

レシートには、Lime Green Latex Paint（ライムグリーンラテックス塗料）、Cordless Drill（コードレスドリル）、Hammer（ハンマー）などの商品が記載されているので、そのような商品を販売しているホームセンターで発行されたことがわかる。よって、(B)が正解。

🎧 2-15 🇬🇧

156.

What is NOT included on the receipt?
(A) A transaction number
(B) The payment method
(C) The time of purchase
(D) A fee for shipping

レシートに含まれていないのはどれですか。
(A) 取引番号
(B) 支払い方法
(C) 購入時刻
(D) 配送料金

▶ 正解　(D)

(A) A transaction number（取引番号）はTransaction: 24558が、(B) The payment method（支払い方法）はPayment method: OVC Credit Cardが、(C) The time of purchase（購入時刻）はSeptember 18 (3:02 P.M.)がそれぞれ該当する。(D) A fee for shipping（配送料金）は記載されていないので、これが正解。

157.

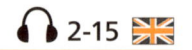

Which item cannot be returned to Ratcliff & Sons?
(A) The lime green latex paint
(B) The cordless drill
(C) The hammer
(D) The paint roller

Ratcliff & Sonsに返品できないのはどの品物ですか。
(A) ライムグリーンラテックス塗料
(B) コードレスドリル
(C) ハンマー
(D) 塗装用ローラー

▶ 正解　(A)

レシートの下方にall paints and paint-related products, except for rollers, are non-refundable and cannot be returned to the store for exchange or store credit.（ローラーを除き、全ての塗料と塗装関連製品は、返金不可で交換やストアクレジットによる返品をお受けできない）とあるので、塗料である(A) The lime green latex paint（ライムグリーンラテックス塗料）は返品できないことがわかる。よって、(A)が正解。

Questions 158–160 refer to the following article.

1文書：記事

🎧 2-16 🇬🇧

ARC Hotels Group Announces Plans for Expansion of Coral Bay Resort

Wellington, NZ (23 January)—The ARC Hotels Group has announced plans to expand its Coral Bay resort. The development will include the addition of forty-eight rooms, two restaurants, and a shopping arcade featuring 1,800 square meters of retail space. — [1] —.

The decade-old resort was built next to Anders Grove Golf Club, which ARC purchased last year. — [2] —. The expansion will be constructed on a tract of land adjacent to the golf course.

"Coral Bay has transformed from a quiet coastal village to a tourist hotspot," said Harvey Carter, President, ARC Hotels Group. "Years ago, we saw this change coming, and we wanted our resort there to have more dining options and guest rooms. — [3] —. After purchasing Anders Grove, however, we now have enough land to make it bigger and even better."

The ARC Hotels Group owns 256 hotels around the world, including two in New Zealand. — [4] —. It was founded in 1968 by Samuel Cooper, a businessman who made his fortune in the steel industry. ARC plans to debut its expanded Coral Bay resort in December.

問題158～160は次の記事に関するものです。

ARC Hotels Groupが、Coral Bayリゾートの拡張計画を発表

Wellington、ニュージーランド（1月23日）──ARC Hotels Groupは、同社のCoral Bayリゾートを拡張する計画を発表した。拡張計画は、48の客室、2軒のレストラン、そして1,800平方メートルの小売スペースを持つショッピングアーケードの追加を含む。

開業10年のリゾートは、ARCが昨年買収したAnders Grove Golf Clubの隣に建設された。拡張部分は、ゴルフコースに隣接する広大な土地に建設される。

「Coral Bayは、のどかな沿岸集落から旅行者に人気のスポットへと変化を遂げました」と、ARC Hotels Groupの社長であるHarvey Carterは述べた。「何年も前に、私たちはこの変化の到来を予期し、そこにある私たちのリゾートがより多くの食事処と客室を持てればと思っていました。当時は、場所が足りず、それは不可能でした。しかし、私たちはAnders Groveを購入したので、今やリゾートをより大きく、よりよくするために十分な土地を所有しています。」

ARC Hotels Groupは、ニュージーランドの2軒を含み、世界各地に256軒のホテルを所有している。それは、鉄鋼産業で富を築いた実業家のSamuel Cooperによって、1968年に設立された。ARCは、拡張されたCoral Bayの営業開始を12月に予定している。

- announce 動 発表する
- expansion 名 拡張
- expand 動 拡張する
- development 名 開発
- square meters 平方メートル
- retail 形 小売の
- decade-old 形 10年の月日が経った
- purchase 動 買収する
- construct 動 建設する
- tract of land 広大な土地、一区画の土地
- adjacent to ～の隣に
- transform 動 変化する
- coastal 形 沿岸の
- tourist hotspot 人気観光スポット
- found 動 設立する
- fortune 名 富、財産

158. 🎧 2-16

What is the article mainly about?
(A) Construction of a golf course
(B) Tourists from overseas
(C) Additions to a resort
(D) Cooperation between two companies

主に何についての記事ですか。
(A) ゴルフコースの建設
(B) 海外からの観光客
(C) リゾートの増築
(D) 2社間の提携

▶ 正解 (C)

この記事はリゾートホテルの拡張計画を伝えているので、(C)が正解。全体の内容を把握して答えを選ぶ問題だが、見出しのARC Hotels Group Announces Plans for Expansion of Coral Bay Resort や本文の初めのThe ARC Hotels Group has announced plans to expand its Coral Bay resort. (ARC Hotels Groupは、同社のCoral Bayリゾートを拡張する計画を発表した) などがヒントとなる。

- construction 名 建設
- from overseas 海外から
- addition 名 増築

▶ 言い換えポイント Expansion of Coral Bay Resort ➡ Additions to a resort

159. 🎧 2-16

What is reported about the ARC Hotels Group?
(A) It plans to open a second hotel on Coral Bay.
(B) It will renovate its headquarters in December.
(C) It is still managed by the founder.
(D) It owns more than one hotel in New Zealand.

ARC Hotels Groupについて何が報告されていますか。
(A) Coral Bayに2軒目のホテルを開く予定である。
(B) 12月に本社を改装する。
(C) 今でも創業者によって経営されている。
(D) ニュージーランドに複数のホテルを所有している。

▶ 正解 (D)

The ARC Hotels Group owns 256 hotels around the world, including two in New Zealand. (ARC Hotels Groupは、ニュージーランドの2軒を含み、世界各地に256軒のホテルを所有している) とあるので、(D)が正解。

- renovate 動 改装する
- headquarters 名 本社
- founder 名 創業者

▶ 言い換えポイント two in New Zealand ➡ more than one hotel in New Zealand

160.

In which of the positions marked [1], [2], [3], and [4] does the following sentence best belong?

"At the time, this was impossible due to lack of space."

(A) [1]
(B) [2]
(C) [3]
(D) [4]

[1]、[2]、[3]、[4]と記載された箇所のうち、次の文が入るのに最もふさわしいのはどれですか。

「当時は、場所が足りず、それは不可能でした」

(A) [1]
(B) [2]
(C) [3]
(D) [4]

▶ 正解　(C)

At the time, this was impossible due to lack of space.（当時は、場所が足りず、それは不可能でした）を [3] の位置に入れると、this が前の文の we wanted our resort there to have more dining options and guest rooms.（そこにある私たちのリゾートがより多くの食事処と客室を持てればと思っていました）を受けることになり、上手くつながる。

Questions 161–163 refer to the following information.

Space Available for Rehearsals

Are you looking for a studio to prepare for a performance? Our spacious Sanctum Studio is available to rent by the hour and is conveniently located near the theater district.

Perfect for rehearsals and photo shoots, Sanctum Studio is larger than the average dance studio. Its lobby provides additional space for a piano or other instruments brought to the building.

This multipurpose space also has state-of-the-art sound and lighting equipment and two dressing rooms, which can be used at no additional cost.

DETAILS

Location: 86 Madison Street, Jarviston
Phone: 555-2864

Studio parking: 18-vehicle lot (included in rental rate)
Public parking: parking lot across the street

Pricing: The rate varies depending on the time and day the space is used (standard rate: $45.00 per hour).

A discount is given to students attending Markford College.

To see photographs of Sanctum Studio or to reserve the space online, visit: www.sanctumstudio.org.

問題161〜163は次の情報に関するものです。

リハーサルに利用可能なスペース

公演に向けて準備するためのスタジオをお探しですか。広々としたSanctum Studioは、時間単位でのレンタルが可能で、劇場地区付近の便利な場所にあります。

リハーサルや写真撮影に最適なSanctum Studioは、平均的なダンススタジオより広くなっています。ロビーは建物に持ち込まれるピアノや他の楽器のためのスペースを提供します。

この多目的スペースは、追加料金なしでご利用いただける最新の音響および照明機器と2つの更衣室も備えています。

詳細
住所：86 Madison Street, Jarviston
電話：555-2864

スタジオ専用駐車場：18台収容駐車場（レンタル料金に含む）
公共駐車場：駐車場は通りの向かい

ご利用料金：料金は、ご利用の日時により異なります（標準料金：1時間あたり45ドル）。

Markford Collegeに通う学生には割引があります。

Sanctum Studioの写真をご覧になる、またはスペースをオンラインで予約するには、www.sanctumstudio.org.にアクセスしてください。

- □ **spacious** 形 広々とした
- □ **conveniently located** 便利な場所にある
- □ **perfect for ~** ～に最適な
- □ **instrument** 名 楽器
- □ **multipurpose** 形 多目的の
- □ **state-of-the-art** 形 最新の
- □ **at no additional cost** 追加料金なしで
- □ **lot** 名 駐車場
- □ **pricing** 名 価格設定
- □ **vary** 動 変わる
- □ **attend** 動 通う
- □ **reserve** 動 予約する

Part 7 | 解答・解説

161. 🎧 2-17 🇬🇧

What is implied about Sanctum Studio?
(A) It is ideal for practices.
(B) Its Web site will be redesigned.
(C) It is usually busy in the evening.
(D) It is the largest dance studio in Jarviston.

Sanctum Studioについて何が示唆されていますか。
(A) 練習に理想的である。
(B) ウェブサイトのデザインが変更になる。
(C) 夜は通常、混み合う。
(D) Jarvistonで最大のダンススタジオである。

▶ **正解 (A)**

第2段落にPerfect for rehearsals and photo shoots（リハーサルや写真撮影に最適）とあるので、(A) It is ideal for practices.（練習に理想的である）が正解。

▶ **言い換えポイント** Perfect for rehearsals ➡ ideal for practices

162. 🎧 2-17 🇬🇧

What is NOT mentioned as being covered by the rental fee?
(A) Modern equipment
(B) Changing rooms
(C) Parking spaces
(D) Musical instruments

レンタル料金に含まれると述べられていないのはどれですか。
(A) 最新器材
(B) 更衣室
(C) 駐車場
(D) 楽器

▶ **正解 (D)**

第3段落のThis multipurpose space also has state-of-the-art sound and lighting equipment and two dressing rooms, which can be used at no additional cost.（この多目的スペースは、追加料金なしでご利用いただける最新の音響および照明機器と2つの更衣室も備えています）から、(A)と(B)が無料で利用できることがわかり、右側のStudio parking: 18-vehicle lot (included in rental rate)（スタジオ専用駐車場：18台収容駐車場（レンタル料金に含む））から、(C)も料金に含まれていることがわかる。楽器の貸出に関する記述はないので、(D)が正解。

▶ **言い換えポイント** state-of-the-art ➡ Modern
dressing rooms ➡ Changing rooms

163. 🎧 2-17 🇬🇧

According to the information, what is across the street from Sanctum Studio?
(A) A university
(B) A parking lot
(C) A movie theater
(D) A public park

情報によれば、Sanctum Studioの通りの向かい側には何がありますか。
(A) 大学
(B) 駐車場
(C) 映画館
(D) 公共の公園

▶ **正解 (B)**

右側上段にPublic parking: parking lot across the street（公共駐車場：駐車場は通りの向かい）とあるので、(B)が正解。

Questions 164–167 refer to the following form.

Phoenix Grocers
CUSTOMER SERVICE QUESTIONNAIRE

Phoenix Grocers is looking for new ways to make our customers even happier. That is why we want to know how you feel about us. Please take a moment to rate each statement in the list on a scale of 1 to 4, where 1 = strongly agree, 2 = agree, 3 = disagree, and 4 = strongly disagree.

If you include your name and phone number, you will be entered in a drawing for a chance to win 100 dollars' worth of groceries from our store!

Name: Shania Winston   **Phone:** 555-3857

Statement	1	2	3	4
Phoenix offers more variety than other local supermarkets.	①	2	3	4
Phoenix prices are fair compared to those of other supermarkets.	1	②	3	4
The produce at Phoenix is always fresh.	①	2	3	4
Phoenix employees are helpful.	1	②	3	4
Phoenix shelves are well organized.	①	2	3	4
There is enough space in the checkout area for bagging groceries.	1	2	③	4
I would recommend Phoenix to others.	1	②	3	4
Overall, I am satisfied as a Phoenix customer.	1	②	3	4

Comments: I regularly visit this supermarket and have noticed it's gotten busier over the years. Getting groceries here used to take 15 minutes, but now it takes half an hour or so. If I were in charge, I'd make space for two more registers.

問題164～167は次の用紙に関するものです。

Phoenix Grocers
お客様アンケート

Phoenix Grocersでは、お客様によりいっそう喜んでいただく新しい方法を探しております。 そのため、皆様が当店についてどのようにお感じになっているかお聞きしたいと思います。少しだけお時間をいただき、リストの各文を次の4段階で評価していただけますでしょうか。1 ＝ 非常にそう思う、2 ＝ そう思う、3 ＝ そう思わない、4 ＝ 全くそう思わない

お名前とお電話番号をご記入いただくと、100ドル分の食品が当たる抽選にエントリーされます。

お名前：Shania Winston　　　電話：555-3857

Phoenixは、他の地元のスーパーより品揃えがよい。	①	2	3	4
Phoenixの価格は、他のスーパーの価格と比較して適正である。	1	②	3	4
Phoenixの青果は、常に新鮮である。	①	2	3	4
Phoenixの従業員は、親切である。	1	②	3	4
Phoenixの商品棚は、きちんと整理されている。	①	2	3	4
レジ付近には、袋詰めをするための十分なスペースがある。	1	2	③	4
Phoenixを他の人々に推薦する。	1	②	3	4
全体的に、Phoenixの顧客として満足している。	1	②	3	4

コメント：私は定期的にこのスーパーを訪れていますが、年月を重ねるにつれて混雑するようになってきたと感じています。食品購入は、以前は15分ですみましたが、現在では30分程度かかります。もし私が責任者だったら、レジをもう2台置くスペースを作るでしょう。

- □ grocer　名 食料品店（= grocery store, supermarket）、食料品店主
- □ questionnaire　名 アンケート　　□ take a moment to ～　少し時間をとって～する
- □ rate　動 評価する　　□ statement　名 文　　□ on a scale of 1 to 4　1から4の段階で
- □ be entered in a drawing　抽選にエントリーされる　　□ compared to ～　～に比べて
- □ produce　名 青果　　□ bag　動 袋詰めにする　　□ recommend　動 推薦する
- □ satisfied　形 満足した　　□ notice　動 気付く

164.

How will Phoenix Grocers most likely use the information it receives on the form?
(A) To determine which products to promote
(B) To increase customer satisfaction
(C) To improve its marketing efforts
(D) To identify hard-working employees

Phoenix Grocersは、用紙で集めた情報をおそらくどのように使いますか。
(A) どの製品を宣伝するか決める
(B) 顧客満足度を上げる
(C) マーケティング活動を向上させる
(D) 勤勉な従業員を特定する

▶ 正解 (B)

冒頭、Phoenix Grocers is looking for new ways to make our customers even happier.（Phoenix Grocersでは、お客様によりいっそう喜んでいただく新しい方法を探しております）と述べ、そのためにアンケートの質問項目に答えるよう頼んでいる。よって、集めた情報は顧客満足度向上に使われることが推測できるので、(B)が正解。

- determine 動 決める
- promote 動 販売促進する
- improve 動 向上させる
- identify 動 特定する

▶ 言い換えポイント make our customers even happier ➡ increase customer satisfaction

165.

What does Ms. Winston indicate on the form?
(A) The selection of products is poor.
(B) Some vegetables are usually sold out.
(C) More shelves should be installed.
(D) There is not enough space in an area.

Winstonさんは、用紙で何を示していますか。
(A) 商品の品揃えが悪い。
(B) いくつかの野菜がたいてい売り切れている。
(C) より多くの棚が設置されるべきである。
(D) あるエリアに十分なスペースがない。

▶ 正解 (D)

Winstonさんは、There is enough space in the checkout area for bagging groceries.（レジ付近には、袋詰めをするための十分なスペースがある）に対して、3 = disagreeの評価をしている。これはレジ付近におけるスペースが不十分であることを示しているので、(D)が正解。

- selection 名 品揃え
- install 動 設置する

166.

What can be inferred about Ms. Winston?
(A) She walks fifteen minutes to the store every day.
(B) She feels that more cashiers are needed.
(C) She decided not to participate in a drawing.
(D) She prefers to shop at other stores.

Winstonさんについて何が推測できますか。
(A) 毎日、15分歩いて店へ行く。
(B) より多くのレジ係が必要であると感じている。
(C) 抽選には参加しないことに決めた。
(D) 他の店で買い物をすることを好む。

▶ 正解 (B)

WinstonさんはコメントにIf I were in charge, I'd make space for two more registers.（もし私が責任者だったら、レジをもう2台置くスペースを作るでしょう）と書いている。これは、レジを増やしてより多くのレジ係が業務にあたれば、客の待ち時間が今より短くなるという提案である。よって、(B)が正解。

- decide 動 決める
- participate in ~ ~に参加する
- prefer 動 より好む

▶ 言い換えポイント I'd make space for two more registers.
➡ She feels that more cashiers are needed.

167.

How has Phoenix Grocers changed?
(A) It offers fewer products.
(B) Its aisles are narrower.
(C) It serves more customers.
(D) Its bags are smaller.

Phoenix Grocersはどのように変わりましたか。
(A) より少ない商品を提供している。
(B) 通路がより狭くなっている。
(C) より多くの顧客にサービスを提供している。
(D) より小さい袋を使っている。

▶ 正解 (C)

Winstonさんはコメント欄にI regularly visit this supermarket and have noticed it's gotten busier over the years.（私は定期的にこのスーパーを訪れていますが、年月を重ねるにつれて混雑するようになってきたと感じています）と書いている。これは、来客数が増えたということなので、(C)が正解。

▶ 言い換えポイント　it's gotten busier ➡ It serves more customers.

□ aisle 名 通路

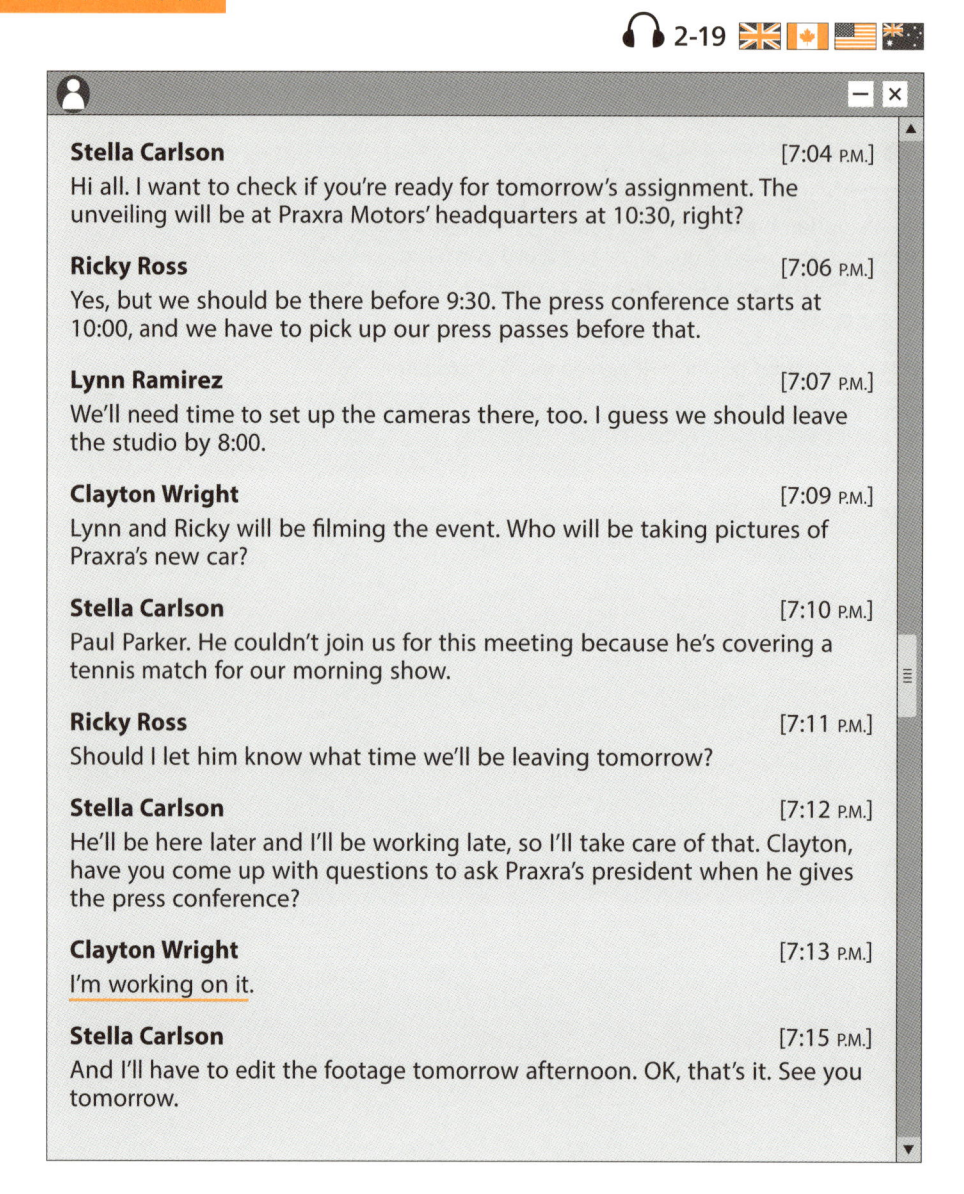

Questions 168–171 refer to the following online chat discussion.

Stella Carlson [7:04 P.M.]
Hi all. I want to check if you're ready for tomorrow's assignment. The unveiling will be at Praxra Motors' headquarters at 10:30, right?

Ricky Ross [7:06 P.M.]
Yes, but we should be there before 9:30. The press conference starts at 10:00, and we have to pick up our press passes before that.

Lynn Ramirez [7:07 P.M.]
We'll need time to set up the cameras there, too. I guess we should leave the studio by 8:00.

Clayton Wright [7:09 P.M.]
Lynn and Ricky will be filming the event. Who will be taking pictures of Praxra's new car?

Stella Carlson [7:10 P.M.]
Paul Parker. He couldn't join us for this meeting because he's covering a tennis match for our morning show.

Ricky Ross [7:11 P.M.]
Should I let him know what time we'll be leaving tomorrow?

Stella Carlson [7:12 P.M.]
He'll be here later and I'll be working late, so I'll take care of that. Clayton, have you come up with questions to ask Praxra's president when he gives the press conference?

Clayton Wright [7:13 P.M.]
I'm working on it.

Stella Carlson [7:15 P.M.]
And I'll have to edit the footage tomorrow afternoon. OK, that's it. See you tomorrow.

問題168～171は次のオンライン・チャットの話し合いに関するものです。

Stella Carlson　　　　　　　　　　　　　　　　　　　　　　　　　　　　　　　　　　［午後7時4分］
では、皆さん、明日の仕事の準備ができているか確認したいと思います。除幕式はPraxra Motorsの本社で10時30分ですね。

Ricky Ross　　　　　　　　　　　　　　　　　　　　　　　　　　　　　　　　　　　　［午後7時6分］
はい、でも9時30分までにそこに着かなければなりません。記者会見は10時から始まるので、その前に取材許可証を受け取る必要があります。

Lynn Ramirez　　　　　　　　　　　　　　　　　　　　　　　　　　　　　　　　　　　［午後7時7分］
そこでカメラを設置する時間も必要になります。8時までにはスタジオを出たほうがいいかなと思います。

Clayton Wright　　　　　　　　　　　　　　　　　　　　　　　　　　　　　　　　　　［午後7時9分］
LynnとRickyは、イベントを撮影します。誰がPraxraの新モデルの車の写真を撮ることになっていますか。

Stella Carlson　　　　　　　　　　　　　　　　　　　　　　　　　　　　　　　　　　［午後7時10分］
Paul Parkerです。彼は、朝の番組のためにテニスの試合を取材しているので、この会議には参加できませんでした。

Ricky Ross　　　　　　　　　　　　　　　　　　　　　　　　　　　　　　　　　　　　［午後7時11分］
明日の出発時間を私が彼に知らせましょうか。

Stella Carlson　　　　　　　　　　　　　　　　　　　　　　　　　　　　　　　　　　［午後7時12分］
彼は後でここに来ますし、私は遅くまで仕事をするつもりなので、私がそれを引き受けます。Clayton、Praxraの社長が記者会見を行う際に尋ねる質問は考えましたか。

Clayton Wright　　　　　　　　　　　　　　　　　　　　　　　　　　　　　　　　　　［午後7時13分］
今、やっているところです。

Stella Carlson　　　　　　　　　　　　　　　　　　　　　　　　　　　　　　　　　　［午後7時15分］
それと、私は明日の午後に映像を編集しなければなりません。さて、以上です。明日会いましょう。

- □ be ready for ～　～の準備ができている　　□ assignment 名 仕事　　□ unveiling 名 除幕式
- □ press conference 記者会見　　□ press pass 取材許可証　　□ cover 動 取材する
- □ edit 動 編集する　　□ footage 名 映像

168.

🎧 2-19

For what type of organization do the writers most likely work?
(A) A conference center
(B) A news agency
(C) A sports arena
(D) A car manufacturer

書き手は、おそらくどんな種類の組織で働いていますか。
(A) 会議施設
(B) 通信社
(C) 競技施設
(D) 自動車メーカー

▶ **正解 (B)**

午後7時6分のThe press conference starts at 10:00, and we have to pick up our press passes before that.(記者会見は10時から始まるので、その前に取材許可証を受け取る必要があります)から、このやりとりを行っている人たちは、(B) A news agency (通信社)で働いていると考えられる。また、filming the event (イベントを撮影します)やI'll have to edit the footage (私は映像を編集しなければなりません)などもヒントとなる。

169.

🎧 2-19

According to the discussion, what will Mr. Parker do tomorrow?
(A) Work late
(B) Take pictures
(C) Edit videos
(D) Ask questions

話し合いによれば、Parkerさんは明日何をしますか。
(A) 遅くまで働く
(B) 写真を撮る
(C) ビデオを編集する
(D) 質問をする

▶ **正解 (B)**

午後7時9分のWho will be taking pictures of Praxra's new car?(誰がPraxraの新モデルの車の写真を撮ることになっていますか)に対する答えがPaul Parkerなので、Parkerさんは次の日に写真を撮ることになっているとわかる。よって、(B)が正解。

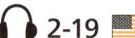

170.

🎧 2-19

When will the president of Praxra Motors speak?
(A) At 8:00
(B) At 9:30
(C) At 10:00
(D) At 10:30

Praxra Motorsの社長は、いつ話しますか。
(A) 8時に
(B) 9時30分に
(C) 10時に
(D) 10時30分に

▶ **正解 (C)**

前半、記者会見が10時からあることが述べられている。そして、午後7時12分のClayton, have you come up with questions to ask Praxra's president when he gives the press conference?(Clayton、Praxraの社長が記者会見を行う際に尋ねる質問は考えましたか)から、Praxra Motorsの社長が記者会見を行うことがわかる。記者会見を行うということは、そこで話をすることを意味するので、社長が話すのは10時である。

171.

At 7:13 P.M., what does Mr. Wright mean when he writes, "I'm working on it"?
(A) He has not finished preparing questions.
(B) He is editing a story about a tennis match.
(C) He is unable to answer Ms. Carlson's question.
(D) He will submit a document later today.

午後7時13分に、Wrightさんが書いている "I'm working on it" は、何を意味していますか。
(A) 質問を準備し終えていない。
(B) テニスの試合についての記事を編集中である。
(C) Carlsonさんの質問に答えられない。
(D) 今日の後ほど書類を提出する。

▶ 正解　(A)

午後7時12分のClayton, have you come up with questions to ask Praxra's president when he gives the press conference? (Clayton、Praxraの社長が記者会見を行う際に尋ねる質問は考えましたか) を受けて、Wrightさんは、I'm working on it. (今、やっているところです) と答えている。それは、その作業がまだ終わっていないことを意味するので、(A) が正解。

Questions 172–175 refer to the following letter.

February 16

Dr. Annette Weisman
Ceres Institute of Botany Research
935 Hillcrest Road
Glendora, CA 91741

Global Nutrition Research Conference

Dear Dr. Weisman:

On behalf of the Global Nutrition Research Conference (GNRC) committee, it is my pleasure to invite you to participate as a speaker at our event this year. — [1] —. The GNRC will be held in Zurich, Switzerland at the Kallendorf Hotel from June 12 to 15.

Nutrition experts from around the world will gather at the GNRC to discuss a broad range of topics related to the theme "Nutrition for a Healthier Tomorrow." Your research on nutrients in mushrooms that was recently published in the journal *Agricultural Science and Sustainability* will be of interest to many conference attendees. — [2] —.

In addition, your former colleague, Dr. Farida Patel, will give a presentation at the GNRC. On the second day of the event, she will discuss her research on a species of mushroom newly discovered in India. Should you also agree to participate, we will schedule your talk for the following day. — [3] —.

Enclosed you will find a conference information package for invited speakers, which contains a description of the conference and its goals, a guest speaker registration form, our speaker compensation policy, and information about hotels and transportation. — [4] —. If you are interested in being a speaker at the conference, please complete the form and send it to the GNRC Committee Office by March 22.

Yours sincerely,

Dennis Hancock

Dennis Hancock
Executive Director
Global Nutrition Research Conference

問題172～175は次の手紙に関するものです。

2月16日

Annette Weisman博士
Ceres Institute of Botany Research
935 Hillcrest Road
Glendora, CA 91741

Weisman博士

Global Nutrition Research Conference (GNRC) 委員会を代表して、今年のイベントに講演者としてご参加いただくようお願いできることは、私にとって喜ばしい事であります。GNRCは、スイスのZurichにあるKallendorf Hotelで6月12日から15日まで開催されます。

「より健康的な未来のための栄養学」というテーマに関連した幅広い範囲のトピックを論じるため、世界中から栄養学の専門家がGNRCに集まります。『Agricultural Science and Sustainability』誌に最近発表されたあなたのキノコの栄養素に関する研究は、多くの学会参加者の関心を呼ぶでしょう。さらに、それは学会のテーマにもよく合っています。

加えて、あなたの元の同僚であるFarida Patel博士が、GNRCで発表を行います。イベントの2日目に、彼女は、インドで新しく発見されたキノコの一種に関する研究について発表します。あなたも参加することに同意していただけるのなら、あなたの講演をその翌日に入れるようにいたします。

同封された招待講演者用の学会情報一式には、学会の説明とその目的、招待講演者の登録用紙、講演者の報酬規程、そしてホテルと交通機関に関する情報が含まれています。この学会の講演者になることにご興味をお持ちいただけましたら、用紙にご記入の上、3月22日までにGNRC委員会事務局にお送りください。

敬具

Dennis Hancock

Dennis Hancock
事務局長
Global Nutrition Research Conference

- □ botany 名 植物学　　on behalf of ～ ～を代表して　　□ nutrition 名 栄養学
- □ committee 名 委員会　　□ invite 動 招待する　　□ participate 動 参加する
- □ hold 動 催す　　□ expert 名 専門家　　□ gather 動 集まる　　□ discuss 動 論じる
- □ a broad range of ～ 幅広い～　　□ related to ～ ～に関連した　　theme 名 テーマ
- □ nutrient 名 栄養素　　□ publish 動 発表する　　□ be of interest to ～ ～の関心を呼ぶ
- □ attendee 名 出席者　　□ in addition 加えて　　□ colleague 名 同僚
- □ a species of ～ ～の一種　　□ discover 動 発見する　　□ schedule 動 予定に入れる
- □ Enclosed you will find ～ ～が同封されている　　□ description 名 説明
- □ registration form 登録用紙　　compensation 名 報酬　　□ complete 動 記入する

172.

🎧 2-20 🇬🇧

When does Mr. Hancock want Dr. Weisman to speak at the event?
(A) On June 12
(B) On June 13
(C) On June 14
(D) On June 15

Hancockさんは、いつWeisman博士にイベントで講演してもらうことを望んでいますか。
(A) 6月12日に
(B) 6月13日に
(C) 6月14日に
(D) 6月15日に

▶ 正解 (C)

6月12日から15日に開催される栄養学の学会の2日目にWeisman博士の元同僚のPatel博士が口頭発表を行うことが述べられ、Should you also agree to participate, we will schedule your talk for the following day. (あなたも参加することに同意していただけるのなら、あなたの講演をその翌日に入れるようにいたします)と続くので、この手紙の書き手のHancockさんはWeisman博士の講演を学会3日目の6月14日に入れるつもりであることがわかる。

173.

🎧 2-20 🇬🇧

What is NOT being sent with the letter?
(A) A conference schedule
(B) Accommodation information
(C) The objectives of the event
(D) A document for registration

手紙と共に送られていないのはどれですか。
(A) 学会日程
(B) 宿泊施設の情報
(C) イベントの目的
(D) 登録のための書類

▶ 正解 (A)

(B)はinformation about hotels and transportation (ホテルと交通機関に関する情報)に、(C)はa description of the conference and its goals (学会の説明とその目的)に、(D)はa guest speaker registration form (招待講演者の登録用紙)にそれぞれ該当する。これらは手紙に同封されているa conference information package (学会情報一式)に含まれている。学会日程に関する記述はないので、(A)が正解。

☐ **accommodation** 名 宿泊施設
☐ **objective** 名 目的

174.

🎧 2-20 🇬🇧

What is Dr. Weisman asked to do?
(A) Continue her research in another country
(B) Collaborate with a former colleague
(C) Review an article in a scientific journal
(D) Return a document to a committee

Weisman博士は何をするよう頼まれていますか。
(A) 別の国で研究を続ける
(B) 元同僚と協力する
(C) 科学雑誌で論文の論評を行う
(D) 委員会に書類を返送する

▶ 正解 (D)

最後にIf you are interested in being a speaker at the conference, please complete the form and send it to the GNRC Committee Office by March 22. (この学会の講演者になることにご興味をお持ちいただけましたら、用紙にご記入の上、3月22日までにGNRC委員会事務所にお送りください)とあるので、(D)が正解。

☐ **continue** 動 続ける
☐ **collaborate** 動 協力する
☐ **review** 動 論評する

▶ 言い換えポイント complete the form and send it to the GNRC Committee Office
➡ Return a document to a committee

175.

In which of the positions marked [1], [2], [3], and [4] does the following sentence best belong?

"Moreover, it fits well with the conference theme."

(A) [1]
(B) [2]
(C) [3]
(D) [4]

[1]、[2]、[3]、[4]と記載された箇所のうち、次の文が入るのに最もふさわしいのはどれですか。

「さらに、それは学会のテーマにもよく合っています」

(A) [1]
(B) [2]
(C) [3]
(D) [4]

▶ 正解 (B)

この文を[2]の位置に入れると、it fits well with the conference theme.（それは学会のテーマにもよく合っています）のit が前の文のYour research on nutrients in mushrooms（あなたのキノコの栄養素に関する研究）を受けることになり、上手くつながる。

☐ **moreover** 副 さらに
☐ **fit** 動 合う

Questions 176–180 refer to the following form and letter.

STAR PARKING
Corner of Lincoln Avenue and Eagle Road

RENTAL AGREEMENT

Owner: Barry Klein
Telephone: 555-9346
Address: 894 Eagle Road, Albertville, MN 55301

Renter: Heidi Welch
Telephone: 555-3867
Address: 9689 Lincoln Avenue, Albertville, MN 55301

The owner agrees to rent Star Parking space __12-F__ to the renter on a month-to-month basis. Prior to each rental month, the renter will pay the rental fee of $50.00 to the owner by check or in cash. The owner will issue a receipt stating the amount paid. In addition to the rental fee, the renter will pay a deposit of $50.00 at the time of signing this agreement. After the final rental month, the owner will return the deposit by check to the renter if no outstanding rent is due. The owner is not responsible for the vehicle while it is parked in the designated space.

Date of agreement: October 29
Signature of owner: Barry Klein
Signature of renter: Heidi Welch

問題176～180は次の用紙と手紙に関するものです。

Star Parking
Lincoln Avenue と Eagle Road の角

賃貸契約書

賃貸人：Barry Klein
電話　：555-9346
住所　：894 Eagle Road, Albertville, MN 55301

貸借人：Heidi Welch
電話　：555-3867
住所　：9689 Lincoln Avenue, Albertville, MN 55301

賃貸人は、Star Parking の 12-F 区画を賃借人に月極めで賃貸することに同意する。各賃貸月の前に、賃借人は小切手または現金で賃貸人に賃貸料50ドルを支払う。賃貸人は、支払われた金額を明記した領収書を発行する。賃借人は、賃貸料に加えて、この契約書に署名する時点で50ドルの保証金を支払う。最終賃貸月後に、未払いの賃料がなければ、賃貸人は賃借人に小切手で保証金を返還する。賃貸人は、車両が指定場所に駐車されている間、車両に対する責任を負わない。

契約日　　　：　10月29日
賃貸人署名：　Barry Klein
賃借人署名：　Heidi Welch

- □ rental agreement　賃貸契約書　　□ rent　動 賃貸する、賃借する　　□ renter　名 賃借人
- □ on a month-to-month basis　月極めで　　□ prior to ～　～の前に　　□ check　名 小切手
- □ issue　動 発行する　　□ state　動 明記する　　□ deposit　名 保証金、敷金
- □ outstanding　形 未払いの　　□ due　形 支払われるべき
- □ responsible for ～　～に対して責任がある　　□ designate　動 指定する

❷ 手紙

🎧 2-21 🇬🇧

March 27

Barry Klein
894 Eagle Road
Albertville, MN 55301

Dear Mr. Klein:

I currently rent space 12-F at Star Parking. I have accepted a job in Vermont and will move to Burlington on April 30; therefore, the enclosed payment for rental of the space will be my last.

As of May 1, my home address will be 412 Cherry Street, Burlington, VT 05401. Since I will be leaving Albertville on April 30, please mail the check for fifty dollars to my new address.

Thank you for always ensuring that the parking lot remains clear of snow in the winter and well lit at night year-round.

Best regards,

Heidi Welch

Heidi Welch

3月27日

Barry Klein
894 Eagle Road
Albertville, MN 55301

Klein様

私は、現在Star Parkingの12-F区画を借りております。私はVermontでの仕事を引き受けたので、4月30日にBurlingtonへ移る予定です。従って、同封した駐車場所の賃借に対する支払いが最後となります。

5月1日以降、私の自宅の住所は、412 Cherry Street, Burlington, VT 05401になります。私は4月30日にAlbertvilleを去る予定ですので、私の新しい住所に50ドルの小切手をお送りください。

いつも駐車場を、冬には雪がなく、夜間は年間を通して明るくしていただき、ありがとうございました。

敬具

Heidi Welch

Heidi Welch

- □ **currently** 副 現在
- □ **accept** 動（採用のオファーを）受ける
- □ **enclose** 動 同封する
- □ **payment** 名 支払い
- □ **as of ～** ～以降は
- □ **ensure** 動 確実にする
- □ **remain** 動 ある状態のままでいる
- □ **well lit** 明るい
- □ **year-round** 副 年間を通して

176. 🎧 2-21

According to the agreement, what did Mr. Klein do on October 29?
(A) He borrowed a vehicle from Ms. Welch.
(B) He made a deposit at a local bank branch.
(C) He agreed to rent out a parking space.
(D) He distributed some parking permits.

契約書によれば、Kleinさんは、10月29日に何をしましたか。
(A) Welchさんから車両を借りた。
(B) 地元の銀行の支店で預金した。
(C) 駐車場所を賃貸することに同意した。
(D) 駐車許可証を配布した。

▶ **正解** (C)

契約書の本文の初めにThe owner agrees to rent Star Parking space 12-F to the renter on a month-to-month basis.（賃貸人は、Star Parkingの12-F区画を賃借人に月極めで賃貸することに同意する）とあり、またその上の部分のOwner: Barry Kleinから、The ownerはKleinさんのことであるとわかるので、「駐車場所を賃貸することに同意した」という(C)が正解。

- □ **make a deposit** 預金する
- □ **rent out** 貸し出す
- □ **distribute** 動 配布する
- □ **permit** 名 許可証

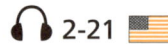

177. 🎧 2-21

What information is NOT included in the agreement?
(A) The date it was signed
(B) The responsibilities of an owner
(C) The location of a parking lot
(D) The role of a parking attendant

契約書に記載されていないのは、どの情報ですか。
(A) 署名された日付
(B) 所有者の責任
(C) 駐車場の場所
(D) 駐車場係員の役割

▶ **正解** (D)

(A)はDate of agreement: October 29（契約日：10月29日）に、(B)はThe owner will issue a receipt stating the amount paid.（賃貸人は、支払われた金額を明記した領収書を発行する）やthe owner will return the deposit by check to the renter（賃貸人は賃借人に小切手で保証金を返還する）に、(C)はStar Parking space 12-F（Star Parkingの12-F区画）にそれぞれ該当する。駐車場係員の役割に関する記述はないので、(D)が正解。

- □ **attendant** 名 係員

Part 7 | 解答・解説

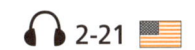

178. 🎧 2-21 🇺🇸

What is one purpose of the letter?
(A) To request information
(B) To accept a job offer
(C) To end an agreement
(D) To explain a resignation

手紙の目的の1つは何ですか。
(A) 情報を要請すること
(B) 職へのオファーを受け入れること
(C) 契約を打ち切ること
(D) 辞職を説明すること

▶ 正解 (C)

手紙の第1段落後半に the enclosed payment for rental of the space will be my last. (同封した駐車場所の賃借に対する支払いが最後となります) とあり、これは契約を打ち切ることを意味するので、(C)が正解。

□ end 動 打ち切る
□ explain 動 説明する
□ resignation 名 辞任

179. 🎧 2-21 🇺🇸

What does Ms. Welch want Mr. Klein to send?
(A) An agreement
(B) A job description
(C) A receipt
(D) A deposit

Welchさんは、Kleinさんに何を送ってもらうことを望んでいますか。
(A) 契約書
(B) 職務内容説明書
(C) 領収書
(D) 保証金

▶ 正解 (D)

手紙の第2段落後半の please mail the check for fifty dollars to my new address. (私の新しい住所に50ドルの小切手をお送りください) から、WelchさんはKleinさんに50ドルの小切手を送ることを求めているのがわかる。また、契約書には署名時に50ドルの保証金を払い、解約時に返金されることが記されているので、この50ドルは保証金であることがわかる。よって、(D)が正解。

180. 🎧 2-21 🇺🇸

Why does Ms. Welch thank Mr. Klein?
(A) He removed snow from her car.
(B) He told her about a job.
(C) A receipt was sent on time.
(D) An area is always bright at night.

WelchさんはなぜKleinさんに感謝していますか。
(A) 彼が彼女の車の雪かきをした。
(B) 彼が彼女に仕事について話した。
(C) 領収書が期日通りに送られた。
(D) ある場所が夜間は常に明るい。

▶ 正解 (D)

手紙の最後に Thank you for always ensuring that the parking lot remains clear of snow in the winter and well lit at night year-round. (いつも駐車場を、冬には雪がなく、夜間は年間を通して明るくしていただき、ありがとうございました) とある。この well lit at night year-round (夜間は年間を通して明るく) を An area is always bright at night. (ある場所が夜間は常に明るい) で言い換えた(D)が正解。

□ remove 動 除く

▶ 言い換えポイント　well lit ➡ bright

153

Questions 181–185 refer to the following memo and report.

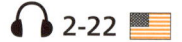

To: All Factory Personnel
Date: April 8
Subject: Factory Checks

On May 12, the Health Department will carry out an inspection of the factory. This will involve a thorough evaluation of our procedures, storage areas, and food processing machinery. The inspection will get underway at 10:00 A.M. and will be completed by around 12:30 P.M.

Beginning next week, supervisor Kylie Henderson will be checking each section of the factory to identify any machinery that will have to be repaired before May 12.

Please note that she will also be observing employees to make sure they are following these standard procedures:

- cleaning all surfaces in contact with food;
- storing cleaners in the appropriate places;
- wearing protective clothing as required; and
- reporting any problems with equipment to supervisors.

Any questions you have regarding the inspection or Ms. Henderson's assessment should be directed to your supervisor. Thank you for your cooperation.

Claude Keegan
Quality Control Manager
Bistros Biscuits, Ltd.

- 食物と接触する全ての表面を清潔にすること。
- 洗浄剤を適切な場所に置いておくこと。
- 定められた通りに防護服を着用すること。
- 機器に関するどんな問題も主任に報告すること。

検査またはHendersonさんの評価に関する質問は、あなたの上司に尋ねてください。ご協力ありがとうございます。

Claude Keegan
品質管理マネージャー
Bistros Biscuits, Ltd.

- ☐ **carry out** 行う ☐ inspection 名 検査 ☐ involve 動 含む ☐ **thorough** 形 徹底した
- ☐ evaluation 名 評価 ☐ procedure 名 手順、作業工程 ☐ storage 名 倉庫
- ☐ process 動 加工する ☐ get underway 始まる ☐ complete 動 完了させる
- ☐ supervisor 名 主任、監督官 ☐ identify 動 特定する
- ☐ please note that ～　～をご留意ください ☐ observe 動 よく見る
- ☐ standard procedure 標準手順 ☐ clean 動 清潔にする ☐ surface 名 表面
- ☐ in contact with ～　～と接触する ☐ **store** 動 保管する ☐ protective 形 防護の
- ☐ as required 定められた通り ☐ regarding 前 ～に関して ☐ assessment 名 評価、査定
- ☐ be directed to ～　～に向けられる ☐ quality control 品質管理

❷ 報告書

🎧 2-22 🇬🇧

Results of Pre-Inspection Check

ASSESSMENT PERIOD: April 14 to April 23
OBSERVER: Kylie Henderson

SUMMARY

All areas of the facility and procedures were observed over a ten-day period, during which the observer identified a total of three problems requiring immediate corrective action:

  I. A component on a dough mixer was broken. This had been known to some workers, but because the machine was still able to function satisfactorily, no one notified a supervisor about the problem.

  II. A countertop was not sanitized after use.

  III. An employee was not wearing protective gloves near the ovens.

This report details these findings and provides guidance for avoiding these problems.

— Page 1 —

検査前点検の結果

評価期間：4月14日から4月23日
視察者　：Kylie Henderson

概要
施設の全ての区域と手順は10日間に渡り視察が行われ、その期間中、視察者は即時の是正措置を必要とする計3件の問題を特定した。

I. 生地用ミキサーの部品が壊れていた。これは一部の作業員には知られていたが、機械がまだ十分機能していたため、誰も問題について主任に知らせなかった。
II. 調理台が使用後、消毒されていなかった。
III. 1人の従業員が、オーブンの近くで保護手袋を着用していなかった。

この報告書は調査結果を詳述し、これらの問題を回避するための指針を示す。

— 1ページ —

- observer 名 視察者
- facility 名 施設
- immediate 形 迅速な、即時の
- corrective 形 正すための
- component 名 部品
- dough 名 生地
- function 動 機能する
- satisfactorily 副 十分に
- notify 動 知らせる
- countertop 名 調理台
- sanitize 動 消毒する
- detail 動 詳しく述べる
- guidance 名 指導
- avoid 動 回避する、避ける

181. 🎧 2-22

What is the purpose of the memo?
(A) To clarify a new procedure
(B) To recommend some changes
(C) To describe some results
(D) To share the details of a plan

連絡メモの目的は何ですか。
(A) 新しい手順を明確にすること
(B) 変更を提言すること
(C) 結果を説明すること
(D) 計画の詳細を共有すること

▶ 正解 (D)

連絡メモは、衛生局の検査に備え、事前に内部点検を行うことを告げ、その詳細を説明している。よって、(D) To share the details of a plan（計画の詳細を共有すること）が正解。

- clarify 動 明確にする
- recommend 動 提言する
- describe 動 記述する

182. 🎧 2-22

Who should employees contact if they have a question about the inspection?
(A) An inspector
(B) A Health Department official
(C) Their supervisor
(D) The quality control manager

従業員が検査に関して質問がある場合、誰に連絡すべきですか。
(A) 検査官
(B) 衛生局の職員
(C) 上司
(D) 品質管理マネージャー

▶ 正解 (C)

連絡メモの終わりにAny questions you have regarding the inspection or Ms. Henderson's assessment should be directed to your supervisor.（検査またはHendersonさんの評価に関する質問は、あなたの上司に尋ねてください）とあるので、(C) が正解。

▶ 言い換えポイント (Any questions) should be directed to ➡ employees contact

183.

Why was the report created?
(A) To alert employees about some problems
(B) To assist inspectors in their work
(C) To compare several different methods
(D) To report on the progress of a project

報告書はなぜ作成されましたか。
(A) 問題に対して従業員に注意を喚起するため
(B) 検査官の仕事を支援するため
(C) 異なる方法を比較するため
(D) プロジェクトの進捗を報告するため

▶ **正解** (A)

報告書では、概要で3件の問題点が示され、また、文末のThis report details these findings and provides guidance for avoiding these problems.(この報告書は調査結果を詳述し、これらの問題を回避するための指針を示す) から、2ページ以降に問題点の詳しい説明と解決方法が記されていると推測できる。よって、(A)が正解。

- □ **alert** 動 注意を喚起する
- □ **compare** 動 比較する
- □ **report on ~** ~について報告する

184.

What can be inferred about the mixer?
(A) It was not checked by Ms. Henderson.
(B) It has to be replaced immediately.
(C) It will be repaired before May 12.
(D) It has not been used since March.

ミキサーについて何が推測できますか。
(A) Hendersonさんによって点検されなかった。
(B) すぐに交換される必要がある。
(C) 5月12日より前に修理される。
(D) 3月から使用されていない。

▶ **正解** (C)

報告書に示されている問題点の初めの項目にA component on a dough mixer was broken.(生地用ミキサーの部品が壊れていた)とある。また、連絡メモにsupervisor Kylie Henderson will be checking each section of the factory to identify any machinery that will have to be repaired before May 12.(Kylie Henderson主任が、5月12日より前に修理すべき機械を特定するために工場の各セクションを点検していきます)とある。よって、壊れているミキサーの部品は5月12日までに修理されるとわかるので、(C)が正解。

- □ **infer** 動 推測する
- □ **replace** 動 交換する

185.

Which standard procedure is NOT mentioned in the report?
(A) Cleaning surfaces
(B) Storing cleaners properly
(C) Wearing protective clothing
(D) Reporting equipment problems

報告書で言及されていないのは、どの標準手順ですか。
(A) 表面を消毒すること
(B) 洗浄剤を適切に保管すること
(C) 防護服を着用すること
(D) 機器の問題を報告すること

▶ **正解** (B)

報告書に記述がない標準手順を選ぶ。(A)はA countertop was not sanitized after use.(調理台が使用後、消毒されていなかった)に、(C)はAn employee was not wearing protective gloves near the ovens.(1人の従業員が、オーブンの近くで保護手袋を着用していなかった)に、(D)はno one notified a supervisor about the problem.(誰も問題について主任に知らせなかった)にそれぞれ該当する。洗浄剤に関する記述はないので、(B)が正解。

Questions 186–190 refer to the following Web page, advertisement, and e-mail.

3文書：❶ ウェブページ

🎧 2-23 🇬🇧

http://www.rexstuxedos.com

Rex's Tuxedo Rentals

| Home | Tuxedos | Accessories | Fitting | About |

Rex's offers contemporary and traditional tuxedos to suit every style. And we are excited to announce that the hottest new styles of tuxedos have been introduced to our rental lineup!

Domino Dayton
- A comfortable tuxedo with a shiny, eye-catching jacket

Antigua Dream
- A great choice for any formal occasion and our only tuxedo in light blue

Panther Padfield
- A classy tuxedo designed by Sal Duval to make you feel like a celebrity

Burgundy Brawn
- A soft blend of wool and cashmere and an all-around fun tuxedo

For more information about these new fashions and our other tuxedos, click here.

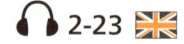

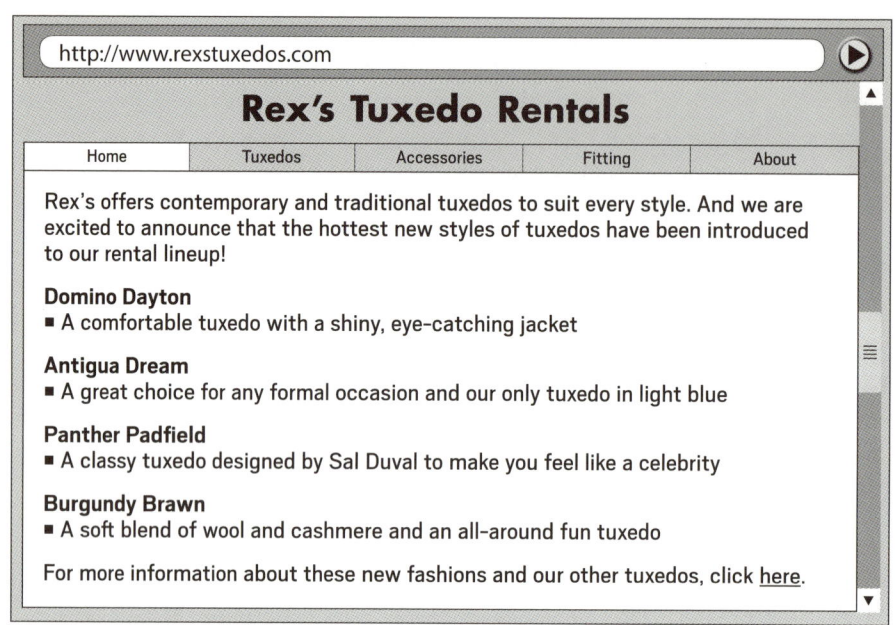

問題186〜190は次のウェブページ、広告、Eメールに関するものです。

http://www.rexstuxedos.com

Rex's Tuxedo Rentals

| ホーム | タキシード | 小物 | 試着 | 当店について |

Rex'sは、あらゆるスタイルに合う、現代的なタキシードと伝統的なタキシードを提供いたします。そして、当店のレンタルのラインナップに、タキシードの最も人気のある新しいスタイルが追加されたことを喜んでお知らせします。

Domino Dayton
■ 光沢があって人目を引くジャケットの、着心地のよいタキシード

Antigua Dream
■ どんなフォーマルな催しにもとても合う、当店唯一のライトブルーのタキシード

Panther Padfield
■ あなたを有名人のような気分にさせる、Sal Duvalのデザインのお洒落なタキシード

Burgundy Brawn
■ ウールとカシミヤの柔らかい混紡織物の、どんな場面にでも合う遊び心のあるタキシード

これらの新しいファッションと当店の他のタキシードの詳細については、ここをクリックしてください。

- □ contemporary 形 現代的な　□ traditional 形 伝統的な　○ suit 動 合う
- □ excited 形 興奮した　□ hot 形 人気のある　□ introduce 動 売り出す、追加する
- □ lineup 名 品揃え　□ comfortable 形 着心地のよい　□ shiny 形 輝く、光沢のある

Part 7 | 解答・解説

- eye-catching 形 人目を引く
- formal 形 フォーマルな、正式の
- occasion 名 場面
- classy 形 洒落た、高級な
- celebrity 名 有名人
- blend 名 混紡織物、混合
- cashmere 名 カシミヤ

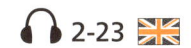

❷ 広告

🎧 2-23 🇬🇧

Rex's Tuxedo Rentals

Need a tuxedo for a wedding, formal dinner, prom, or red carpet event? Find the latest tuxedo fashions and accessories at Rex's Tuxedo Rentals. We offer unbeatable prices, personal service, and onsite alterations. Plus, we give discounts to customers who rent four or more tuxedos at once…

- ▸ Rent 4 tuxedos and get 10% off!
- ▸ Rent 5 to 7 tuxedos and get 15% off!
- ▸ Rent 8 to 10 tuxedos and get 20% off!
- ▸ Rent 11 or more tuxedos and get 25% off!

Got a question? Call us at 555-7545 or come by our shop.
We're at 418 Wilshire Boulevard.

Rex's Tuxedo Rentals

結婚式、晩餐会、卒業記念ダンスパーティーやレッドカーペットイベントのためにタキシードが必要ですか。Rex's Tuxedo Rentals で、最新のタキシードファッションと小物を見つけてください。当店は、他店に負けない価格、お客様一人一人に対応したサービスと店内での寸法直しを行っています。さらに、一度に4着以上のタキシードをレンタルしていただけるお客様には、割引をいたします。

・タキシード4着のレンタルで、10%割引。
・タキシード5〜7着のレンタルで、15%割引。
・タキシード8〜10着のレンタルで、20%割引。
・タキシード11着以上のレンタルで、25%割引。

ご質問はありますか。555-7545までお電話いただくか、店にお越しください。
当店は、418 Wilshire Boulevardにあります。

- prom 名 卒業記念ダンスパーティー
- latest 形 最新の
- unbeatable 形 負けない
- onsite 形 施設内での
- alteration 名 (衣服の)寸法直し
- at once 一度に

159

❸ E メール

🎧 2-23 🇺🇸

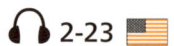

From:	Richard Hicks
To:	Don Lawrence
Re:	Tux Rentals
Date:	April 2

Hello Don,

I hope you enjoyed the awards dinner last night. Although the technical award went to another group of engineers, the fact that we were nominated is an honor in itself. Moreover, the software we created has gained recognition as a result of the nomination, which will be good for sales.

If you visit the Web site for the event, you can see a photo of us seated at the table. We must have caught the photographer's attention because the tablecloths were the same shade of light blue that we were wearing.

Today, I have to bring the tuxedos I rented for the team back to Rex's Tuxedo Rentals. John, Barry, and Leroy brought theirs to my apartment. Ryan and Ted left theirs at the office, so I'll pick those up on my way to Rex's. I also want to stop by your place for the one you wore, so I can return all seven together.

Please let me know if you are going to be home at around four o'clock.

Thank you,

Richard

送信者：Richard Hicks
宛先　：Don Lawrence
件名　：タキシードのレンタル
日付　：4月2日

こんにちは、Don

昨晩の受賞晩餐会を楽しんだことでしょう。技術賞は別のエンジニアのグループが取りましたが、私たちがノミネートされたこと自体が名誉です。さらに、私たちが作ったソフトがノミネートされたことで認識を得たので、それは売上に貢献するでしょう。

イベントのウェブサイトにアクセスすると、私たちがテーブルで席についている写真が見られます。テーブルクロスが、私たちの着ていたライトブルーと同じ色合いだったので、カメラマンの注意を引いたに違いありません。

今日、私はチームのために借りたタキシードをRex's Tuxedo Rentalsに返却しなければなりません。John、BarryとLeroyは、私のアパートにタキシードを持ってきました。RyanとTedは、彼らのタキシードをオフィスに置いて行ったので、Rex'sへ行く途中に私が取りに行きます。7着全てまとめて返却できるように、あなたが着たタキシードを取りにあなたの所にも寄りたいと思っています。

あなたが4時頃に家にいるかどうか知らせてください。

ありがとうございます。

Richard

Part 7 | 解答・解説

- □ technical 形 技術の   □ nominate 動 ノミネートする   □ honor 名 名誉
- □ gain recognition 認識を得る   □ as a result of ~ ~の結果として
- □ nomination 名 ノミネート   □ catch one's attention 注意を引く   □ shade 名 色合い
- □ stop by 立ち寄る   □ return 動 返却する

186. 🎧 2-23 🇬🇧

What has Rex's Tuxedo Rentals announced?
(A) It has new types of outfits.
(B) Its location has changed.
(C) Its opening hours were reduced.
(D) It has hired a new tailor.

Rex's Tuxedo Rentalsは、何を発表していますか。
(A) 新しいタイプの衣服がある。
(B) 店の場所が変わった。
(C) 営業時間が短縮された。
(D) 新しいテーラーを雇った。

▶ 正解 (A)

ウェブページにAnd we are excited to announce that the hottest new styles of tuxedos have been introduced to our rental lineup!（そして、当店のレンタルのラインナップに、タキシードの最も人気のある新しいスタイルが追加されたことを喜んでお知らせします）とあり、新しいタキシードの紹介が続いている。よって、(A)が正解。

- □ outfit 名 衣服
- □ reduce 動 減らす

▶ 言い換えポイント   new styles of tuxedos ➡ new types of outfits

187. 🎧 2-23 🇬🇧

What is indicated about the staff at Rex's Tuxedo Rentals?
(A) They can make adjustments to clothes.
(B) They provide wedding planning services.
(C) They were nominated for an award.
(D) They recently designed some new tuxedos.

Rex's Tuxedo Rentalsの従業員について何がわかりますか。
(A) 服の寸法直しができる。
(B) 結婚式の計画を立てるサービスを提供している。
(C) 賞の候補にノミネートされた。
(D) 最近いくつかの新しいタキシードをデザインした。

▶ 正解 (A)

広告にWe offer unbeatable prices, personal service, and onsite alterations.（当店は、他店に負けない価格、お客様一人一人に対応したサービスと店内での寸法直しを行っています）とある。店内で寸法直しを行うということは、この店の従業員がそれをすることになるので、(A)が正解。

- □ adjustment 名 調整、変更
- □ provide 動 提供する
- □ recently 副 最近

▶ 言い換えポイント   alterations ➡ adjustments to clothes

188.

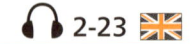

What type of tuxedo did Mr. Hicks wear to the event?
(A) Domino Dayton
(B) Antigua Dream
(C) Panther Padfield
(D) Burgundy Brawn

Hicksさんは、どのタイプのタキシードをイベントに着ていきましたか。
(A) Domino Dayton
(B) Antigua Dream
(C) Panther Padfield
(D) Burgundy Brawn

▶ 正解 (B)

Eメール第2段落のthe tablecloths were the same shade of light blue that we were wearing.（テーブルクロスが、私たちの着ていたライトブルーと同じ色合いだった）から、Hicksさんが着ていたのはライトブルーのタキシードだったことがわかる。さらにウェブページのAntigua Dreamの説明にA great choice for any formal occasion and our only tuxedo in light blue（どんなフォーマルな催しにもとても合う、当店唯一のライトブルーのタキシード）とあるので、ライトブルーのタキシードはAntigua Dreamであるとわかる。よって、(B)が正解。

189.

What is implied in the e-mail?
(A) Mr. Lawrence has returned a suit already.
(B) Mr. Lawrence is Mr. Hicks' supervisor.
(C) Mr. Hicks and his colleagues developed some software.
(D) Mr. Hicks' office is beside Rex's Tuxedo Rentals.

Eメールで何が示唆されていますか。
(A) Lawrenceさんはスーツをすでに返却した。
(B) LawrenceさんはHicksさんの上司である。
(C) Hicksさんと彼の同僚はソフトを開発した。
(D) HicksさんのオフィスはRex's Tuxedo Rentalsのそばにある。

▶ 正解 (C)

Eメール第1段落のthe software we created has gained recognition as a result of the nomination, which will be good for sales.（私たちが作ったソフトがノミネートされたことで認識を得たので、それは売上に貢献するでしょう）から、(C)が正解であるとわかる。

□ imply 動 示唆する
□ develop 動 開発する

▶ 言い換えポイント　created → developed

190.

What discount did Mr. Hicks probably receive?
(A) 10 percent
(B) 15 percent
(C) 20 percent
(D) 25 percent

Hicksさんはおそらくどの割引を受けましたか。
(A) 10パーセント
(B) 15パーセント
(C) 20パーセント
(D) 25パーセント

▶ 正解 (B)

Eメールの第3段落から、Hicksさんがチームのためにタキシードを7着借りたことがわかる。また、広告のwe give discounts to customers who rent four or more tuxedos at once（一度に4着以上のタキシードをレンタルしていただけるお客様には、割引をいたします）とRent 5 to 7 tuxedos and get 15% off!（タキシード5〜7着のレンタルで、15%割引）から、7着まとめて借りた場合は、15%の割引を受けられることがわかる。よって、(B)が正解。

Questions 191–195 refer to the following e-mail, brochure, and online review.

To:	Heather Clark
From:	Andrew McLean
Date:	Monday, October 3
Re:	Brochure Project

Hello Heather,

Management has just announced that we are recalling one of our microwave ovens. This means we will have to take the information about the item out of the new brochure you are designing, I'm sorry to say. After that, you will have to spread out the other three descriptions and pictures evenly.

Can you take care of page 6 by the end of today? Ideally, we will be able to send the data to the printer tomorrow morning as scheduled.

Best regards,

Andrew
Marketing Department
Olynos Electric

問題191〜195は次のEメール、パンフレット、オンラインレビューに関するものです。

宛先　：Heather Clark
送信者：Andrew McLean
日付　：10月3日、月曜日
件名　：パンフレットのプロジェクト

こんにちは、Heather

経営陣は、当社の電子オーブンレンジ1機種をリコールすると先ほど発表しました。申し訳ありませんが、これはあなたがデザインしている最中の新しいパンフレットからその商品に関する情報を削除しなければならないことを意味します。その後、あなたは他の3機種の商品説明と写真を均等に広げなければなりません。

今日中に6ページ目を処理してもらえますか。予定通り明朝に印刷所にデータを送ることができれば理想的です。

敬具

Andrew
マーケティング部
Olynos Electric

□ brochure 名 パンフレット　　□ management 名 経営陣　　□ announce 動 発表する
□ recall 動 リコールする　　□ microwave oven 電子オーブンレンジ
□ take A out of B　AをBから取り除く　　□ spread out 広げる　　□ description 名 説明
□ evenly 副 均等に　　□ take care of ~　~を処理する　　□ ideally 副 理想的には
□ printer 名 印刷所　　□ as scheduled 予定通りに

❷ パンフレット　　　🎧 2-24 🇬🇧

New from Olynos Electric!

Micraway 8000
This versatile microwave makes cooking super convenient. Functioning as an oven and a grill, the Micraway 8000 gives you many cooking options.

Silver Gallance
Olynos Electric's new microwave has twelve heat options, giving the user more control over cooking and reheating items. Powerful but compact, the Silver Gallance is perfect for the smaller kitchen.

Darico Countertop
With more power, this speedy microwave is great for anyone who always has to eat and run. Its stainless steel exterior and spacious interior makes it easy to clean, and it looks great in any kitchen or café.

Zestbox 6000
Designed to make baking breads and cakes easy, the Zestbox's four fans circulate heat to cook or bake food all the way through. This is Olynos Electric's tallest microwave oven with convection capability.

— Page 6 —

Olynos Electricの新製品

Micraway 8000
この多目的電子オーブンレンジを使えば調理がとても手軽になります。オーブンとしてもグリルとしても機能するので、Micraway 8000は多様な調理方法に使えます。

Silver Gallance
Olynos Electricの新しい電子オーブンレンジには12の加熱オプションがあり、食品の調理と温め直しがさらにやりやすくなります。強力でありながらコンパクトなので、Silver Gallanceは小さめのキッチンに適しています。

Darico Countertop
高出力で短時間調理が可能なこの電子オーブンレンジは、常に急いで食事を済ませなくてはならない方に最適です。そのステンレスの外部と広々とした内部は掃除しやすく、どんなキッチンやカフェに置いても見栄えがします。

Zestbox 6000
パンとケーキを簡単に焼けるように設計されたZestboxの4つのファンは、食品の加熱調理や焼き物の際、熱を循環させ完全に火が通るようにさせます。この機種は、対流機能を備えたOlynos Electric製電子オーブンレンジの中で最も高さがあります。

— 6ページ —

- ☐ **versatile** 形 用途の広い ☐ **perfect for ~** ~に最適の
- ☐ **eat and run** 急いで食事をする ☐ **exterior** 名 外部 ☐ **spacious** 形 広々とした
- ☐ **interior** 名 内部 ☐ **circulate** 動 循環させる
- ☐ **cook all the way through** 中まで十分に火が通る ☐ **convection** 名 （熱の）対流
- ☐ **capability** 名 機能

❸ オンラインレビュー

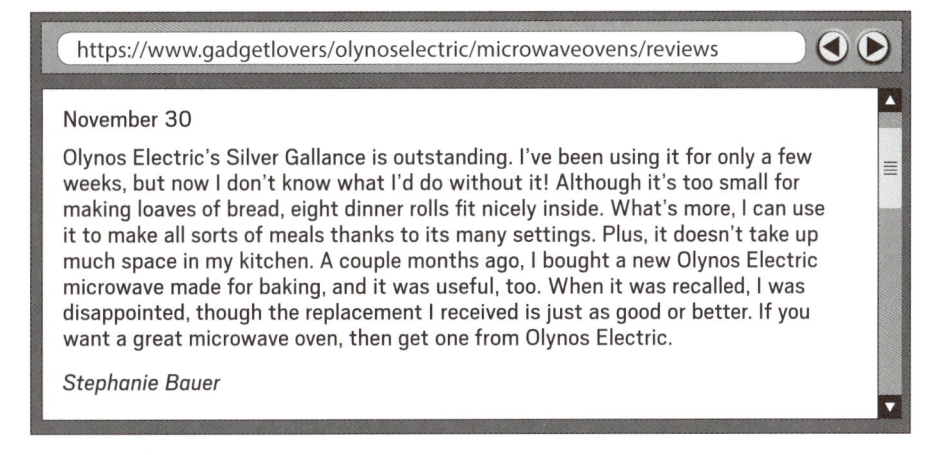

🎧 2-24 🇬🇧

https://www.gadgetlovers/olynoselectric/microwaveovens/reviews

November 30

Olynos Electric's Silver Gallance is outstanding. I've been using it for only a few weeks, but now I don't know what I'd do without it! Although it's too small for making loaves of bread, eight dinner rolls fit nicely inside. What's more, I can use it to make all sorts of meals thanks to its many settings. Plus, it doesn't take up much space in my kitchen. A couple months ago, I bought a new Olynos Electric microwave made for baking, and it was useful, too. When it was recalled, I was disappointed, though the replacement I received is just as good or better. If you want a great microwave oven, then get one from Olynos Electric.

Stephanie Bauer

https://www.gadgetlovers/olynoselectric/microwaveovens/reviews

11月30日

Olynos ElectricのSilver Gallanceは実にすぐれています。私はそれをまだ2、3週間しか使っていませんが、今やそれなしでは何をすればよいかわからないほどです。食パンを焼くには小さ過ぎますが、8個のディナーロールが内部にうまく収まります。その上、多くの設定があるおかげで色々な料理を作るのに使えます。さらに、それは私のキッチンであまり場所を取りません。数ヵ月前、私はパン焼き用に作られた新しいOlynos Electric製電子オーブンレンジを購入しましたが、それも便利でした。それがリコールされた時、私はがっかりしましたが、私が受け取った交換品は同等もしくはそれ以上によい製品です。素晴らしい電子オーブンレンジをお求めであれば、Olynos Electricから購入するのがよいでしょう。

Stephanie Bauer

- ☐ **outstanding** 形 特にすぐれている
- ☐ **loaf of bread** 一斤のパン（焼いてから切っていない 一塊のパン）（複数形は loaves）
- ☐ **thanks to ~** ~のおかげで ☐ **take up** （場所を）取る ☐ **disappointed** 形 がっかりした
- ☐ **replacement** 名 交換品

191.

What is mentioned about Olynos Electric?
(A) One of its products has been recalled.
(B) Some of its employees design kitchens.
(C) It plans to purchase a new printer.
(D) It has announced the opening of a new factory.

Olynos Electricについて何が述べられていますか。
(A) 製品の1つがリコールされた。
(B) 一部の社員はキッチンを設計する。
(C) 新しいプリンターを購入する予定である。
(D) 新しい工場の開設を発表した。

▶ 正解 (A)

Eメールの初めにManagement has just announced that we are recalling one of our microwave ovens.（経営陣は、当社の電子オーブンレンジ1機種をリコールすると先ほど発表しました）とあり、ここでのour microwave ovens（当社の電子オーブンレンジ）はOlynos Electric社の製品を指す。また、オンラインレビューでもOlynos Electric製の電子オーブンレンジがリコールされたことが述べられている。よって、(A)が正解。

192.

Which product has been recalled?
(A) The Micraway 8000
(B) The Silver Gallance
(C) The Darico Countertop
(D) The Zestbox 6000

どの商品がリコールされましたか。
(A) Micraway 8000
(B) Silver Gallance
(C) Darico Countertop
(D) Zestbox 6000

▶ 正解 (D)

オンラインレビューから、パン焼き用に作られた電子オーブンレンジがリコールされたことがわかり、パンフレットのZestbox 6000の欄のDesigned to make baking breads and cakes easy（パンとケーキを簡単に焼けるように設計された）から、この商品がパン焼き用の電子オーブンレンジであることがわかる。よって、(D)が正解。

193.

How is the Darico Countertop microwave oven described?
(A) It is attractive.
(B) It is heavy.
(C) It is tall.
(D) It is compact.

Darico Countertop電子オーブンレンジはどのように説明されていますか。
(A) 魅力的である。
(B) 重い。
(C) 高さがある。
(D) コンパクトである。

▶ 正解 (A)

パンフレットのDarico Countertopの欄にit looks great in any kitchen or café.（どんなキッチンやカフェに置いても見栄えがします）とあり、外観のよさが述べられている。それはIt is attractive.（魅力的である）と言い換えることができるので、(A)が正解。

▶ 言い換えポイント　it looks great ➡ It is attractive.

Part 7 | 解答・解説

🎧 2-24 🇺🇸

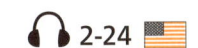

194.

In the online review, the word "outstanding" in paragraph 1, line 1, is closest in meaning to
(A) excellent
(B) unfinished
(C) durable
(D) tall

オンラインレビューの第1段落・1行目のoutstandingに最も意味が近いのは
(A) 素晴らしい
(B) 未完成の
(C) 耐久性がある
(D) 高さがある

▶ 正解 (A)

outstandingは「傑出した、特にすぐれている」、または「未解決の、未払いの」などの意味を持つ形容詞であるが、オンラインレビューの第1段落・1行目では、Olynos Electric's Silver Gallance is outstanding.（Olynos ElectricのSilver Gallanceは実にすぐれています）という商品の説明の中で使われている。よって、(A) excellent（素晴らしい）が正解。「未解決の」の意味であれば、(B) unfinishedが同義語となる。

🎧 2-24 🇺🇸

195.

What is implied in the online review?
(A) Ms. Bauer does not recommend buying Olynos Electric products.
(B) Ms. Bauer is disappointed with her new microwave oven.
(C) The Silver Gallance microwave oven is no longer manufactured.
(D) Olynos Electric replaced Ms. Bauer's microwave oven.

オンラインレビューで何が示唆されていますか。
(A) BauerさんはOlynos Electric製品の購入を勧めない。
(B) Bauerさんは彼女の新しい電子オーブンレンジに失望している。
(C) Silver Gallance電子オーブンレンジはすでに製造中止となっている。
(D) Olynos ElectricはBauerさんの電子オーブンレンジを交換した。

▶ 正解 (D)

オンラインレビューの後半にWhen it was recalled, I was disappointed, though the replacement I received is just as good or better.（それがリコールされた時、私はがっかりしましたが、私が受け取った交換品は同等もしくはそれ以上によい製品です）とあるので、Bauerさんが初めに購入した電子オーブンレンジはリコールされ、代わりとなる交換品が送られてきたことがわかる。交換を行ったのはOlynos Electric社なので、(D)が正解。

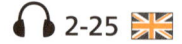

Questions 196–200 refer to the following list, schedule, and e-mail.

Albums by Harris Cassidy

Howling Blue Nights
Unlike his first three blues albums, this latest one by Cassidy includes both blues and jazz. It is arguably his most creative recording and brings together many instruments and styles.

Pond Springs Magic
Featuring the popular song "Dreams on the Breeze" and Burney McRae on the saxophone, this blues album consists of songs with strong rhythms and entertaining lyrics.

Mississippi Amber Moon
Cassidy's best-selling album to date, *Mississippi Amber Moon* is a superb collection of blues songs and includes Cassidy's biggest hit ever "Soul Long."

Songs for the Deluge
The debut album that made Harris Cassidy famous for his outstanding talent on the guitar, *Songs for the Deluge* is now a classic that every blues fan should own.

問題196〜200は次のリスト、スケジュール、Eメールに関するものです。

Harris Cassidyのアルバム

『Howling Blue Nights』
最初の3枚のブルースのアルバムとは異なり、Cassidyのこの最新アルバムは、ブルースとジャズの両方を含んでいる。これはおそらく彼の最も創造的なレコーディングであり、多くの楽器とスタイルを組み合わせている。

『Pond Springs Magic』
人気の曲「Dreams on the Breeze」とBurney McRaeのサックスを目玉とするこのブルースのアルバムは、力強いリズムと面白い歌詞の曲で構成されている。

『Mississippi Amber Moon』
Cassidyのアルバムの中で今日までに最も売れた『Mississippi Amber Moon』は、ブルースの最高のコレクションで、Cassidyのこれまでの最大のヒット曲「Soul Long」が収録されている。

『Songs for the Deluge』
傑出したギターの才能でHarris Cassidyを有名にしたデビューアルバムの『Songs for the Deluge』は、今や全てのブルースファン必携の名作と目されている。

- □ howling　形　吠える
- □ unlike　前　〜とは異なり
- □ latest　形　最新の
- □ include　動　含む
- □ arguably　副　おそらく
- □ creative　形　独創的な
- □ instrument　名　楽器
- □ feature　動　目玉にする
- □ consist of 〜　〜で構成されている
- □ entertaining　形　面白い、楽しませる
- □ lyrics　名　歌詞
- □ amber　形　琥珀の
- □ superb　形　最上の
- □ biggest hit ever　これまでの最大のヒット
- □ outstanding　形　傑出した
- □ classic　名　名作
- □ own　動　所有する

❷ スケジュール

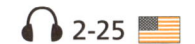

🎧 2-25

```
http://www.brookhavenfestival.org
```

BROOKHAVEN BLUES & JAZZ FESTIVAL

| ABOUT | SCHEDULE | TICKETS | NEWS | VOLUNTEER | CONTACT |

Day One (Saturday, July 19)

Legendary Sheepdogs　2:00–3:40 P.M.
When you combine the mesmerizing voice of Lucille Williams with Gus Reed on the trumpet, you get an exciting yet soothing blend of modern blues. This Alabama band will kick off both days of the festival.

Harris Cassidy　4:00–5:20 P.M.
Considered one of the most talented blues guitarists of all time, Harris Cassidy will play songs from his latest album and of course all of his best-known tunes from the past. This will be an amazing performance, so don't miss it!

The Rusty Nails　5:45–7:10 P.M.
Formed twenty-four years ago, The Rusty Nails have released eleven albums. Known for putting on exciting shows, the band is a must-see for any blues lover. Grab some food at a food stall and enjoy the music!

Daddy Dwyer and the Kings　7:30–9:00 P.M.
If you haven't seen Daddy Dwyer and his band perform, then be ready for a musical experience you'll never forget! Daddy Dwyer and the Kings will close the first day of the festival, which will be immediately followed by a special surprise.

---

http://www.brookhavenfestival.org

BROOKHAVEN BLUES & JAZZ FESTIVAL

| フェスティバルについて | スケジュール | チケット | ニュース | ボランティア | 問い合わせ |

1日目（7月19日、土曜日）

Legendary Sheepdogs　午後2時–3時40分
Lucille Williamsの魅惑の歌声とGus Reedのトランペットが合わさる時、現代のブルースの刺激的かつ心地よい調和が得られます。このAlabamaのバンドが、フェスティバルの両日のスタートを切ります。

Harris Cassidy　午後4時–5時20分
史上最も優れたブルースギタリストの1人と見なされているHarris Cassidyは、最新アルバムの曲と、そしてもちろん過去の最も有名な曲を全て演奏します。素晴らしい演奏となるので、お見逃しなく。

The Rusty Nails　午後5時45分–7時10分
24年前に結成されたThe Rusty Nailsは、11枚のアルバムを発売しています。刺激的なショーを行うことで知られ、ブルース愛好家にとって必見のバンドです。屋台で食べ物を買って、音楽をお楽しみください。

Daddy Dwyer and the Kings　午後7時30分–9時
あなたがDaddy Dwyerと彼のバンドの演奏を見たことがないなら、決して忘れられない音楽の体験になると思ってください。Daddy Dwyer and the Kingsはフェスティバルの初日を締めくくりますが、その後すぐに特別なサプライズが続きます。

- ☐ legendary 形 伝説の　　☐ combine A with B　AとBを合わせる
- ☐ mesmerizing 形 魅惑的な　　☐ soothing 形 癒しの　　☐ kick off 始める
- ☐ best-known 形 最もよく知られている　　☐ amazing 形 素晴らしい　　☐ release 動 発売する
- ☐ must-see 名 必見　　☐ grab 動 つかみ取る、得る　　☐ immediately 副 直ちに
- ☐ follow 動 続く　　☐ surprise 名 サプライズ（内容を知らせずに行われるイベント）

❸ E メール

🎧 2-25

E-Mail Message

From:	<stucker@celeritymail.com>
To:	<organizers@brookhavenfestival.org>
Date:	July 20
Subject:	Music Festival

Thank you for organizing such a fun festival yesterday! The performers were as great as the weather. And the fireworks show at the end was a fantastic addition to this year's event. I had a wonderful time. Unfortunately, however, I lost my watch there. I'm positive that it slipped out of my pocket. And that must have happened during the final performance, which was the only time I sat down on the grass.

If I had noticed it was missing sooner, I would have gone to your information tent inside the venue to let your staff know. Now, I am writing this with the hope that it has been found and was handed over to someone at the tent. If it was, please call me at 555-8994.

Best regards,

Steven Tucker

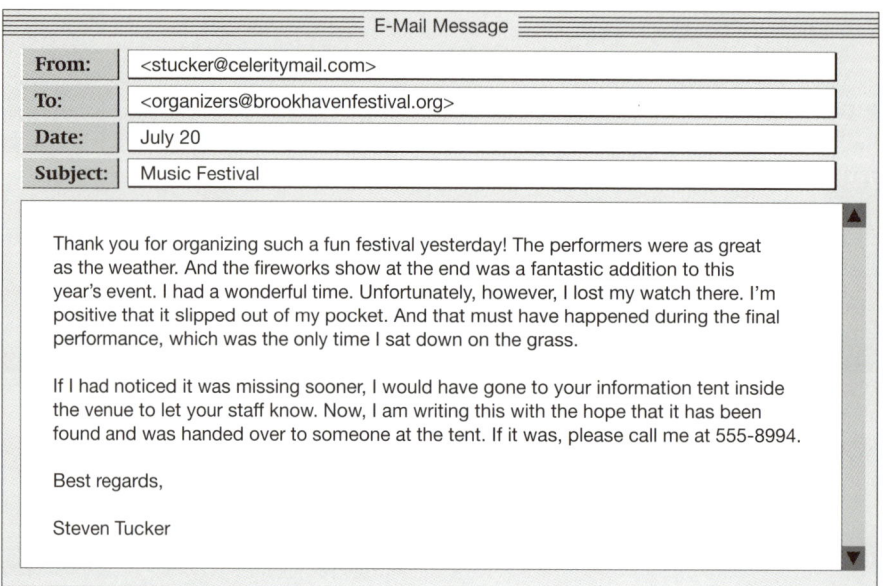

送信者： <stucker@celeritymail.com>
宛先： <organizers@brookhavenfestival.org>
日付： 7月20日
件名： 音楽フェスティバル

昨日はとても楽しいフェスティバルを企画してくださり、ありがとうございました。演奏者は、天気と同様に素晴らしく、最後の花火ショーも今年のイベントに花を添えていました。私は最高の時間が過ごせました。しかし、残念なことに、私はそこで腕時計を失くしてしまいました。ポケットから滑り落ちたのだと確信しています。そしてそれは、私が芝の上に座った唯一の時である最後の演奏の間に起こったに違いありません。

それがなくなっていることにもっと早く気付いていれば、スタッフに知らせるために会場内の案内テントに行ったのですが。今、私はそれが見つかりテントの誰かに手渡されたという望みを持ってこれを書いています。もしそうであれば、555-8994まで私にお電話をください。

敬具

Steven Tucker

Part 7 | 解答・解説

- organize 動 企画する
- fireworks show 花火ショー
- fantastic 形 素晴らしい
- addition 名 追加されたもの
- wonderful 形 素晴らしい
- unfortunately 副 残念なことに
- positive 形 確信して
- slip out of ~ ~から滑り落ちる
- grass 名 芝生
- notice 動 気付く
- missing 形 紛失している
- venue 名 会場

♪ 2-25 🇬🇧

196.

Which Harris Cassidy album features different types of music?

(A) *Howling Blue Nights*
(B) *Pond Springs Magic*
(C) *Mississippi Amber Moon*
(D) *Songs for the Deluge*

Harris Cassidyのどのアルバムが、異なる種類の音楽を収録していますか。

(A)『Howling Blue Nights』
(B)『Pond Springs Magic』
(C)『Mississippi Amber Moon』
(D)『Songs for the Deluge』

▶ 正解 (A)

リストの第1項目 *Howling Blue Nights* の説明に Unlike his first three blues albums, this latest one by Cassidy includes both blues and jazz.（最初の3枚のブルースのアルバムとは異なり、Cassidyのこの最新アルバムは、ブルースとジャズの両方を含んでいる）とあるので、(A) が正解。

▶ 言い換えポイント　includes both blues and jazz
　　　　　　　　　➡ features different types of music

♪ 2-25 🇬🇧

197.

What is probably true about Harris Cassidy's performance at the festival?

(A) He performed the song "Soul Long."
(B) Burney McRae performed with him.
(C) It was the first musical performance.
(D) It did not end until after 7:10 P.M.

フェスティバルでのHarris Cassidyの演奏についておそらく正しいのはどれですか。

(A)「Soul Long」という曲を演奏した。
(B) Burney McRaeが一緒に演奏した。
(C) それが最初の音楽の演奏だった。
(D) それは午後7時10分までには終わらなかった。

▶ 正解 (A)

スケジュールのHarris Cassidyの欄に Harris Cassidy will play songs from his latest album and of course all of his best-known tunes from the past.（Harris Cassidyは、最新アルバムの曲と、そしてもちろん過去の最も有名な曲を全て演奏します）とあり、リストの *Mississippi Amber Moon* の説明に Cassidy's biggest hit ever "Soul Long."（Cassidyのこれまでの最大のヒット曲「Soul Long」）とあるので、彼は「Soul Long」を演奏したと推測できる。よって、(A) が正解。

198.

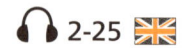

What most likely was the special surprise at the festival?
(A) A fireworks display
(B) A gift bag
(C) A special award
(D) A fifth performer

フェスティバルでの特別なサプライズは、おそらく何でしたか。
(A) 花火ショー
(B) ギフトバッグ
(C) 特別な賞
(D) 5番目の演奏者

▶ 正解　(A)

スケジュールのDaddy Dwyer and the Kingsの欄にDaddy Dwyer and the Kings will close the first day of the festival, which will be immediately followed by a special surprise.（Daddy Dwyer and the Kingsはフェスティバルの初日を締めくくりますが、その後すぐに特別なサプライズが続きます）とあるので、サプライズはその日の最後に行われることがわかる。また、Eメールの前半にthe fireworks show at the end was a fantastic addition to this year's event.（最後の花火ショーも今年のイベントに花を添えていました）とあることから、その日の最後に花火ショーが行われたことがわかる。よって、(A)が正解。

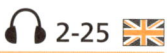

199.

What is the main purpose of the e-mail?
(A) To ask about some procedures
(B) To inquire about a lost item
(C) To express concern about a venue
(D) To confirm receipt of some information

Eメールの主な目的は何ですか。
(A) 手順について尋ねること
(B) 紛失した品物について尋ねること
(C) 会場に対する懸念を示すこと
(D) 情報の受け取りを確認すること

▶ 正解　(B)

Eメールの前半にUnfortunately, however, I lost my watch there.（しかし、残念なことに、私はそこで腕時計を失くしてしまいました）とあり、さらに後半でI am writing this with the hope that it has been found and was handed over to someone at the tent.（私はそれが見つかりテントの誰かに手渡されたという望みを持ってこれを書いています）と述べているので、(B)が正解。

□ receipt　名 受け取ること

200.

Who was most likely performing when Mr. Tucker was sitting down?
(A) Legendary Sheepdogs
(B) Harris Cassidy
(C) The Rusty Nails
(D) Daddy Dwyer and the Kings

Tuckerさんが座っていた時、おそらく誰が演奏していましたか。
(A) Legendary Sheepdogs
(B) Harris Cassidy
(C) The Rusty Nails
(D) Daddy Dwyer and the Kings

▶ 正解　(D)

EメールにAnd that must have happened during the final performance, which was the only time I sat down on the grass.（それは、私が芝の上に座った唯一の時である最後の演奏の間に起こったに違いありません）とあるので、彼が座っていたのは最後の演奏が行われている時である。そして、スケジュールから最後の出演者はDaddy Dwyer and the Kingsであるとわかるので、(D)が正解。

キリトリ線

TOEIC® Listening & Reading Test 標準模試 1
解答用紙

フリガナ	
NAME 氏名	

LISTENING SECTION

Part 1		Part 2						Part 3						Part 4					
No.	ANSWER A B C D	No.	ANSWER A B C	No.	ANSWER A B C	No.	ANSWER A B C D	No.	ANSWER A B C D	No.	ANSWER A B C D	No.	ANSWER A B C D	No.	ANSWER A B C D	No.	ANSWER A B C D	No.	ANSWER A B C D
1	Ⓐ Ⓑ Ⓒ Ⓓ	11	Ⓐ Ⓑ Ⓒ	21	Ⓐ Ⓑ Ⓒ	31	Ⓐ Ⓑ Ⓒ	41	Ⓐ Ⓑ Ⓒ Ⓓ	51	Ⓐ Ⓑ Ⓒ Ⓓ	61	Ⓐ Ⓑ Ⓒ Ⓓ	71	Ⓐ Ⓑ Ⓒ Ⓓ	81	Ⓐ Ⓑ Ⓒ Ⓓ	91	Ⓐ Ⓑ Ⓒ Ⓓ
2	Ⓐ Ⓑ Ⓒ Ⓓ	12	Ⓐ Ⓑ Ⓒ	22	Ⓐ Ⓑ Ⓒ	32	Ⓐ Ⓑ Ⓒ Ⓓ	42	Ⓐ Ⓑ Ⓒ Ⓓ	52	Ⓐ Ⓑ Ⓒ Ⓓ	62	Ⓐ Ⓑ Ⓒ Ⓓ	72	Ⓐ Ⓑ Ⓒ Ⓓ	82	Ⓐ Ⓑ Ⓒ Ⓓ	92	Ⓐ Ⓑ Ⓒ Ⓓ
3	Ⓐ Ⓑ Ⓒ Ⓓ	13	Ⓐ Ⓑ Ⓒ	23	Ⓐ Ⓑ Ⓒ	33	Ⓐ Ⓑ Ⓒ Ⓓ	43	Ⓐ Ⓑ Ⓒ Ⓓ	53	Ⓐ Ⓑ Ⓒ Ⓓ	63	Ⓐ Ⓑ Ⓒ Ⓓ	73	Ⓐ Ⓑ Ⓒ Ⓓ	83	Ⓐ Ⓑ Ⓒ Ⓓ	93	Ⓐ Ⓑ Ⓒ Ⓓ
4	Ⓐ Ⓑ Ⓒ Ⓓ	14	Ⓐ Ⓑ Ⓒ	24	Ⓐ Ⓑ Ⓒ	34	Ⓐ Ⓑ Ⓒ Ⓓ	44	Ⓐ Ⓑ Ⓒ Ⓓ	54	Ⓐ Ⓑ Ⓒ Ⓓ	64	Ⓐ Ⓑ Ⓒ Ⓓ	74	Ⓐ Ⓑ Ⓒ Ⓓ	84	Ⓐ Ⓑ Ⓒ Ⓓ	94	Ⓐ Ⓑ Ⓒ Ⓓ
5	Ⓐ Ⓑ Ⓒ Ⓓ	15	Ⓐ Ⓑ Ⓒ	25	Ⓐ Ⓑ Ⓒ	35	Ⓐ Ⓑ Ⓒ Ⓓ	45	Ⓐ Ⓑ Ⓒ Ⓓ	55	Ⓐ Ⓑ Ⓒ Ⓓ	65	Ⓐ Ⓑ Ⓒ Ⓓ	75	Ⓐ Ⓑ Ⓒ Ⓓ	85	Ⓐ Ⓑ Ⓒ Ⓓ	95	Ⓐ Ⓑ Ⓒ Ⓓ
6	Ⓐ Ⓑ Ⓒ Ⓓ	16	Ⓐ Ⓑ Ⓒ	26	Ⓐ Ⓑ Ⓒ	36	Ⓐ Ⓑ Ⓒ Ⓓ	46	Ⓐ Ⓑ Ⓒ Ⓓ	56	Ⓐ Ⓑ Ⓒ Ⓓ	66	Ⓐ Ⓑ Ⓒ Ⓓ	76	Ⓐ Ⓑ Ⓒ Ⓓ	86	Ⓐ Ⓑ Ⓒ Ⓓ	96	Ⓐ Ⓑ Ⓒ Ⓓ
7	Ⓐ Ⓑ Ⓒ	17	Ⓐ Ⓑ Ⓒ	27	Ⓐ Ⓑ Ⓒ	37	Ⓐ Ⓑ Ⓒ Ⓓ	47	Ⓐ Ⓑ Ⓒ Ⓓ	57	Ⓐ Ⓑ Ⓒ Ⓓ	67	Ⓐ Ⓑ Ⓒ Ⓓ	77	Ⓐ Ⓑ Ⓒ Ⓓ	87	Ⓐ Ⓑ Ⓒ Ⓓ	97	Ⓐ Ⓑ Ⓒ Ⓓ
8	Ⓐ Ⓑ Ⓒ	18	Ⓐ Ⓑ Ⓒ	28	Ⓐ Ⓑ Ⓒ	38	Ⓐ Ⓑ Ⓒ Ⓓ	48	Ⓐ Ⓑ Ⓒ Ⓓ	58	Ⓐ Ⓑ Ⓒ Ⓓ	68	Ⓐ Ⓑ Ⓒ Ⓓ	78	Ⓐ Ⓑ Ⓒ Ⓓ	88	Ⓐ Ⓑ Ⓒ Ⓓ	98	Ⓐ Ⓑ Ⓒ Ⓓ
9	Ⓐ Ⓑ Ⓒ	19	Ⓐ Ⓑ Ⓒ	29	Ⓐ Ⓑ Ⓒ	39	Ⓐ Ⓑ Ⓒ Ⓓ	49	Ⓐ Ⓑ Ⓒ Ⓓ	59	Ⓐ Ⓑ Ⓒ Ⓓ	69	Ⓐ Ⓑ Ⓒ Ⓓ	79	Ⓐ Ⓑ Ⓒ Ⓓ	89	Ⓐ Ⓑ Ⓒ Ⓓ	99	Ⓐ Ⓑ Ⓒ Ⓓ
10	Ⓐ Ⓑ Ⓒ	20	Ⓐ Ⓑ Ⓒ	30	Ⓐ Ⓑ Ⓒ	40	Ⓐ Ⓑ Ⓒ Ⓓ	50	Ⓐ Ⓑ Ⓒ Ⓓ	60	Ⓐ Ⓑ Ⓒ Ⓓ	70	Ⓐ Ⓑ Ⓒ Ⓓ	80	Ⓐ Ⓑ Ⓒ Ⓓ	90	Ⓐ Ⓑ Ⓒ Ⓓ	100	Ⓐ Ⓑ Ⓒ Ⓓ

READING SECTION

Part 5						Part 6				Part 7									
No.	ANSWER A B C D	No.	ANSWER A B C D	No.	ANSWER A B C D	No.	ANSWER A B C D	No.	ANSWER A B C D	No.	ANSWER A B C D	No.	ANSWER A B C D	No.	ANSWER A B C D	No.	ANSWER A B C D	No.	ANSWER A B C D
101	Ⓐ Ⓑ Ⓒ Ⓓ	111	Ⓐ Ⓑ Ⓒ Ⓓ	121	Ⓐ Ⓑ Ⓒ Ⓓ	131	Ⓐ Ⓑ Ⓒ Ⓓ	141	Ⓐ Ⓑ Ⓒ Ⓓ	151	Ⓐ Ⓑ Ⓒ Ⓓ	161	Ⓐ Ⓑ Ⓒ Ⓓ	171	Ⓐ Ⓑ Ⓒ Ⓓ	181	Ⓐ Ⓑ Ⓒ Ⓓ	191	Ⓐ Ⓑ Ⓒ Ⓓ
102	Ⓐ Ⓑ Ⓒ Ⓓ	112	Ⓐ Ⓑ Ⓒ Ⓓ	122	Ⓐ Ⓑ Ⓒ Ⓓ	132	Ⓐ Ⓑ Ⓒ Ⓓ	142	Ⓐ Ⓑ Ⓒ Ⓓ	152	Ⓐ Ⓑ Ⓒ Ⓓ	162	Ⓐ Ⓑ Ⓒ Ⓓ	172	Ⓐ Ⓑ Ⓒ Ⓓ	182	Ⓐ Ⓑ Ⓒ Ⓓ	192	Ⓐ Ⓑ Ⓒ Ⓓ
103	Ⓐ Ⓑ Ⓒ Ⓓ	113	Ⓐ Ⓑ Ⓒ Ⓓ	123	Ⓐ Ⓑ Ⓒ Ⓓ	133	Ⓐ Ⓑ Ⓒ Ⓓ	143	Ⓐ Ⓑ Ⓒ Ⓓ	153	Ⓐ Ⓑ Ⓒ Ⓓ	163	Ⓐ Ⓑ Ⓒ Ⓓ	173	Ⓐ Ⓑ Ⓒ Ⓓ	183	Ⓐ Ⓑ Ⓒ Ⓓ	193	Ⓐ Ⓑ Ⓒ Ⓓ
104	Ⓐ Ⓑ Ⓒ Ⓓ	114	Ⓐ Ⓑ Ⓒ Ⓓ	124	Ⓐ Ⓑ Ⓒ Ⓓ	134	Ⓐ Ⓑ Ⓒ Ⓓ	144	Ⓐ Ⓑ Ⓒ Ⓓ	154	Ⓐ Ⓑ Ⓒ Ⓓ	164	Ⓐ Ⓑ Ⓒ Ⓓ	174	Ⓐ Ⓑ Ⓒ Ⓓ	184	Ⓐ Ⓑ Ⓒ Ⓓ	194	Ⓐ Ⓑ Ⓒ Ⓓ
105	Ⓐ Ⓑ Ⓒ Ⓓ	115	Ⓐ Ⓑ Ⓒ Ⓓ	125	Ⓐ Ⓑ Ⓒ Ⓓ	135	Ⓐ Ⓑ Ⓒ Ⓓ	145	Ⓐ Ⓑ Ⓒ Ⓓ	155	Ⓐ Ⓑ Ⓒ Ⓓ	165	Ⓐ Ⓑ Ⓒ Ⓓ	175	Ⓐ Ⓑ Ⓒ Ⓓ	185	Ⓐ Ⓑ Ⓒ Ⓓ	195	Ⓐ Ⓑ Ⓒ Ⓓ
106	Ⓐ Ⓑ Ⓒ Ⓓ	116	Ⓐ Ⓑ Ⓒ Ⓓ	126	Ⓐ Ⓑ Ⓒ Ⓓ	136	Ⓐ Ⓑ Ⓒ Ⓓ	146	Ⓐ Ⓑ Ⓒ Ⓓ	156	Ⓐ Ⓑ Ⓒ Ⓓ	166	Ⓐ Ⓑ Ⓒ Ⓓ	176	Ⓐ Ⓑ Ⓒ Ⓓ	186	Ⓐ Ⓑ Ⓒ Ⓓ	196	Ⓐ Ⓑ Ⓒ Ⓓ
107	Ⓐ Ⓑ Ⓒ Ⓓ	117	Ⓐ Ⓑ Ⓒ Ⓓ	127	Ⓐ Ⓑ Ⓒ Ⓓ	137	Ⓐ Ⓑ Ⓒ Ⓓ	147	Ⓐ Ⓑ Ⓒ Ⓓ	157	Ⓐ Ⓑ Ⓒ Ⓓ	167	Ⓐ Ⓑ Ⓒ Ⓓ	177	Ⓐ Ⓑ Ⓒ Ⓓ	187	Ⓐ Ⓑ Ⓒ Ⓓ	197	Ⓐ Ⓑ Ⓒ Ⓓ
108	Ⓐ Ⓑ Ⓒ Ⓓ	118	Ⓐ Ⓑ Ⓒ Ⓓ	128	Ⓐ Ⓑ Ⓒ Ⓓ	138	Ⓐ Ⓑ Ⓒ Ⓓ	148	Ⓐ Ⓑ Ⓒ Ⓓ	158	Ⓐ Ⓑ Ⓒ Ⓓ	168	Ⓐ Ⓑ Ⓒ Ⓓ	178	Ⓐ Ⓑ Ⓒ Ⓓ	188	Ⓐ Ⓑ Ⓒ Ⓓ	198	Ⓐ Ⓑ Ⓒ Ⓓ
109	Ⓐ Ⓑ Ⓒ Ⓓ	119	Ⓐ Ⓑ Ⓒ Ⓓ	129	Ⓐ Ⓑ Ⓒ Ⓓ	139	Ⓐ Ⓑ Ⓒ Ⓓ	149	Ⓐ Ⓑ Ⓒ Ⓓ	159	Ⓐ Ⓑ Ⓒ Ⓓ	169	Ⓐ Ⓑ Ⓒ Ⓓ	179	Ⓐ Ⓑ Ⓒ Ⓓ	189	Ⓐ Ⓑ Ⓒ Ⓓ	199	Ⓐ Ⓑ Ⓒ Ⓓ
110	Ⓐ Ⓑ Ⓒ Ⓓ	120	Ⓐ Ⓑ Ⓒ Ⓓ	130	Ⓐ Ⓑ Ⓒ Ⓓ	140	Ⓐ Ⓑ Ⓒ Ⓓ	150	Ⓐ Ⓑ Ⓒ Ⓓ	160	Ⓐ Ⓑ Ⓒ Ⓓ	170	Ⓐ Ⓑ Ⓒ Ⓓ	180	Ⓐ Ⓑ Ⓒ Ⓓ	190	Ⓐ Ⓑ Ⓒ Ⓓ	200	Ⓐ Ⓑ Ⓒ Ⓓ

文法用語まとめ

1. **冠詞**……「冠詞」は名詞の前に置かれ、名詞を限定する。定冠詞theと不定冠詞a/anがある。

2. **前置詞**……「前置詞」は名詞、代名詞、動名詞など、名詞としての働きをする語句の前に置かれる。

3. **形容詞**……「形容詞」は名詞の性質や状況を説明する。名詞を修飾したり、動詞の補語となったりする。

4. **副詞**……「副詞」は主に動詞、形容詞、副詞、副詞句、副詞節、さらに文全体も修飾する。

5. **to不定詞**……「不定詞」は、目的、原因、根拠、結果、条件、程度などを示したり、形容詞のように直前の名詞の具体的な内容を説明したり、名詞のように主語、補語、目的語になったりする。

6. **動名詞**……「動名詞」は動詞のing形で、名詞的に文の主語や目的語、補語になり、動詞的に目的語を持つことができる。
   ※本書では「動名詞」「現在分詞」ともに「動詞の-ing形」として表記している。

7. **現在分詞**……「現在分詞」は動詞の-ing形で、進行形を作り、また形容詞のように名詞を修飾する。

8. **過去分詞**……「過去分詞」は基本的に動詞の-ed形で（不規則動詞は例外）、動詞の完了形、受動態を作り、また形容詞のように名詞を修飾する。

9. **分詞構文**……「分詞構文」は現在分詞または過去分詞が副詞句を作り、文全体を修飾し、時、原因、理由、付帯状況、条件、譲歩などを示す。

10. **関係代名詞**……「関係代名詞」は前の名詞（先行詞）を説明する関係詞節と先行詞を関連付け、接続詞として機能する。関係代名詞にはwho、which、that、whatがある（whatは先行詞を兼ねる）。

11. **関係副詞**……「関係副詞」も関係代名詞と同様に、先行詞を説明する関係詞節と先行詞を結びつける働きをする。関係副詞にはwhen、where、why、howがある。

12. **複合関係詞**……「複合関係詞」は先行詞と関係詞を兼ねる。名詞的に機能する「複合関係名詞」（whoever、whichever、whatever）、形容詞的に機能する「複合関係形容詞」（whatever、whichever）、副詞的に機能する「複合関係副詞」（whenever、wherever、however）がある。

13. **接続詞**……「接続詞」は語と語、句と句、節と節、文と文を結びつける。

14. **句**……「句」は、主語と動詞のない言葉のかたまりで、名詞句、形容詞句、副詞句がある。

15. **節**……「節」は、主語と動詞を含む言葉のかたまりで、名詞節、形容詞節、副詞節がある。

16. **名詞句・名詞節**……「名詞句」と「名詞節」は名詞のように文中で主語、補語、目的語として使われる。

17. **形容詞句・形容詞節**……「形容詞句」と「形容詞節」は形容詞のように文中の名詞や代名詞を修飾する。

18. **副詞句・副詞節**……「副詞句」は副詞の働きをし、文中の動詞、形容詞、副詞、または文全体を修飾する。「副詞節」は副詞の働きをし、文中の動詞や文全体を修飾する。時、場所、原因、理由、目的、結果、条件、譲歩など様々な意味を表す。

19. **目的語**……「目的語」には「動詞の目的語」と「前置詞の目的語」があり、名詞または名詞に相当する語句（動名詞など）が目的語となる。

20. **補語**……「補語」は主語や目的語の状態を説明し、文の成立に必要な語句。

21. **仮定法過去**……「仮定法過去」は現在の事実に反する仮定を表し、動詞は過去形を使う。

22. **仮定法過去完了**……「仮定法過去完了」とは過去の事実に反する仮定を表し、動詞は過去完了形を使う。

23. **仮定法現在**……「仮定法現在」は現在、および未来における仮定、想像、期待、願望、主張、命令、評価、提案、勧誘、要求などを表し、動詞は原形を使う。

神崎正哉 （かんざき・まさや）

1967年、神奈川県生まれ。やどかり出版株式会社代表取締役。神田外語大学講師。東京水産大学（現東京海洋大学）海洋環境工学科卒。テンプル大学大学院修士課程修了（英語教授法）。TOEIC® Listening & Reading Test 990点、TOEIC® Speaking Test 200点、TOEIC® Writing Test 200点、英検1級、国連英検特A級、ケンブリッジ英検CPEなど、英語の資格を多数保持。
著書に『新TOEIC® TEST 出る順で学ぶボキャブラリー990』（講談社）、共著書に『TOEIC® TEST 新形式模試 はじめての挑戦』（小社）、『新TOEIC® TEST パート5特急 400問ドリル』（朝日新聞出版）などがある。
TOEIC学習者のためのブログ、TOEIC Blitz Blog運営：
http://toeicblog.blog22.fc2.com/

Daniel Warriner （ダニエル・ワーリナ）

1974年、カナダ、ナイアガラフォールズ生まれ。ブロック大学英文学科卒。1998年来日。北海道大学、都内の英語学校でTOEIC®テスト対策、英会話を教えるとともに、講師トレーニング及び教材開発に携わる。現在、翻訳会社に勤務。共著書に『1駅1題 新TOEIC® TEST 読解特急』（朝日新聞出版）『はじめての新TOEIC® TEST完全総合対策』（IBCパブリッシング）『TOEIC® TEST 新形式模試 はじめての挑戦』（小社）などがある。

モニター模試協力者の皆さま（敬称略）

愛穂	高橋裕樹	弥勒寺真弓	Osamu
あゆむ	タクミン	めじ	Mich
市川基寿	たけ	山孤	MIMIZU
小川晃司	ちかさん	山之内敏浩	MONO
神 玲子	チャック	ゆ	morchan327
カッキー	ともこ	ゆいいち	nag
木村徹	とらひこ	（50音順）	Pan
きよぱん	西田輝子		Rabbit
くさか のりお	野村信夫	Aki	Rojer
グリーンリッキー	はな	AKKO	SHU.
ぐりん	ぴきい	beatbox	taka
古賀賢一	ビットおじ3	H.H.	Yuji Kawakami
小早川真由美	ひろこ	HANA	zero
さとけい	福井淑永	Kanta	（アルファベット順）
散策	ふじみねこ	KEG	
清水雄大	宮下厚	kkkeiko	
下山智裕	まりこ。	Komachi	
ずーみん	ミルキー	Kumamon	ほか、18名

ご協力とご教示をいただき、どうもありがとうございます。
心より感謝申し上げます。

編集協力
Joe F
Karl Rosvold
及川亜也子
たか
渡邉真理子

音源制作
英語教育協議会（ELEC）
東健一
Hannah Grace 🇺🇸
Howard Colefield 🇺🇸
Nadia McKechnie 🇬🇧
Neil DeMaere 🇨🇦
Stuart O 🇦🇺

Copyright © 2015 Educational Testing Service. www.ets.org
Directions for the TOEIC® Listening and Reading Test are reprinted by permission of Educational Testing Service, the copyright owner. All other information contained within this publication is provided by Yadokari Publishing, Inc. and no endorsement of any kind by Educational Testing Service should be inferred.

TOEIC® LISTENING AND READING TEST
標準模試1

2016年11月30日　第1刷発行

著　者	神崎正哉 Daniel Warriner
装　幀	川原田良一
本文デザイン	コントヨコ
発行者	神崎正哉
発行元	やどかり出版株式会社 yadokari@yadokari-pub.com www.yadokari-pub.com
発売元	IBCパブリッシング株式会社 〒162-0804　東京都新宿区中里町29番3号　菱秀神楽坂ビル9F www.ibcpub.co.jp Tel: 03-3513-4511　Fax: 03-3513-4512
印刷所	株式会社 シナノパブリッシングプレス

©2016 Masaya Kanzaki, Daniel Warriner
Published in Japan by Yadokari Publishing Inc.
ISBN 978-4-7946-0445-3
定価はカバーに表示してあります。
乱丁・落丁本は、発売元にお送りください。送料弊社負担にてお取り替えいたします。
本書の無断複製は著作権法上での例外を除き禁じられています。